Education Without the State

James Tooley

University Research Fellow,
University of Manchester;
Director, IEA Education and Training Unit

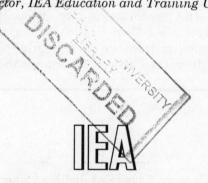
IEA

Published by the
IEA Education and Training Unit

1996

First published in April 1996
by

THE EDUCATION AND TRAINING UNIT
THE INSTITUTE OF ECONOMIC AFFAIRS
2 Lord North Street, Westminster,
London SW1P 3LB

IEA Studies in Education No.1

All Rights Reserved

ISBN 0-255 36380-X

Set in Century Schoolbook and Bookman Old Style

Printed in Great Britain by
Goron Pro-Print Co. Ltd.
Churchill Industrial Estate, Lancing, West Sussex

Contents

Foreword

Few issues are as controversial as education reform. Strong differences of opinions, for instance, concern the causes of poor literacy records, teenage dropouts, inadequate school preparation for job seekers, the appropriate school leaving age, arguments for and against a national curriculum and what to include in it, the rôle of religious education, sex education, 'political awareness' education, and so on.

To a large extent, the wide range of opinion reflects variations amongst people in the kind of society in which they would like to live. And although these preferences are not something that can be subjected to scientific analysis, there remains a confident assumption among professional educationists that, with continual perseverance, they will soon produce the 'one best system', a system, of course, that remains a monopoly within the public sector.

In this stimulating book, James Tooley vigorously challenges the above assumption. Writing at a time of growing support for the introduction of meaningful educational choice for dispersed and heterogeneous family consumers, the author displays a masterly grasp of most of the key aspects of the debate, including the economics, politics, philosophy and educational history. The comprehensive references to the most recent academic and professional literature, right down to 1996, will themselves be a Godsend for those wishing to be thoroughly informed on current controversies.

Tooley argues that, except for the truly indigent, government financial support for education is neither essential nor desirable. With regard to the revisionist history of British education, he concludes that most critics would now agree that the quantity of schooling prior to its collectivisation was substantial but they would strongly disagree about its quality. After careful consideration, however, he is not convinced by the claims of some historians that there were superior standards in publicly inspected schools prior to 1870, one of the reasons being the biased nature of the inspectors' reports.

His involvement in the historical discussion, however, gives Tooley occasion for developing a major new theme. Whereas the historians are speaking primarily of 19th-century *schooling*, the real issue is *education*, and this occurred in a wide variety of places, including formal and informal apprenticeship, communal discussion groups, the availability of newspapers in public houses, coffee houses or reading rooms, the institution of the travelling lecturer, the radical press, the Sunday schools and generally the extended family. Today we should be similarly aware of the even greater potential for decentralised sources of education, as for instance with the new avenue of networking through the internet with influential people around the world. James Tooley's emphasis on the dispersed and unplanned nature of the dynamic of new knowledge creation is clearly inspired by the work of Hayek and it leads him to produce, in Chapter 5, a brilliant challenge to those who enthusiastically support the idea of a national curriculum.

Tooley's book demands especial attention, not only because it ranges over a wide intellectual spectrum but also because it ends with interesting practical policy suggestions. After applauding recent decentralisation reforms such as open-enrolment, *per capita* funding, and local management of schools, the author pushes further by way of his proposed 'Lifelong Individual Fund for Education' (LIFE). Initially the fund would be equivalent to two years' current account spending per head on schooling – around £4,000. At first the LIFE would be available once the student reached the age of 14, while compulsory schooling would finish at that age. Finance for the operation would come from savings elsewhere in the state education system. And if the programme is successful, as Tooley predicts, his idea is to extend it eventually to earlier age groups. Meanwhile the proposal is consistent with his emphasis on the need to allow non-school alternatives to flourish where individual demand calls for it.

This brief summary does not, of course, do justice to the book's carefully crafted details. Readers will not be disappointed when they reach them, and, in general, they will discover that James Tooley has produced a feast of analysis

7

and a vigorous contribution to the debate in terms of economic plus social theory, in addition to interesting practical proposals for political implementation.

March 1996   EDWIN G. WEST
Professor Emeritus of Economics,
Carleton University, Ottawa

COLIN ROBINSON
Editorial Director, Institute of Economic Affairs;
Professor of Economics, University of Surrey

The Author

James Tooley is University Research Fellow at the School of Education, University of Manchester, and is Director of the Education and Training Unit at the Institute of Economic Affairs. His PhD, in philosophy of education, is from the Institute of Education, University of London. Previously, he held research posts at the University of Oxford's Department of Educational Studies and the National Foundation for Educational Research. He also taught courses in philosophy and sociology of education at Homerton College, University of Cambridge; University of East London; University of the Western Cape, South Africa; and Simon Fraser University, Canada. He serves on the Executive Committee of the Philosophy of Education Society of Great Britain. Before entering educational research, he was a mathematics teacher in Zimbabwe and London.

Acknowledgements

Many educationist colleagues have helped me formulate the ideas in this paper. Although most would not agree with the position I have arrived at, all have been courteous and constructive in their criticism. I particularly wish to thank Jan Derry, Antony Flew, Gerald Grace, Arthur Hearnden, Alison Kirton, Meira Levinson, Richard Pring, Peter Pumfrey, Stewart Ranson, Mark Tooley and John White. Very helpful comments on an earlier draft were received from Professor Colin Robinson and two referees. I also owe a considerable debt to Professor E.G. West. Last but not least, thanks to Audrey for loving support throughout.

J.T.

1 | The Question

Why should governments be involved in education? Historically, government intervention, for example in the German states and France, can often be explained in terms of the desire of rulers to build an obedient citizenry for military and industrial might (Richman, 1994, Green, 1990). Perhaps other governments became involved for more benign reasons – but whatever the reasons historically, are there continuing justifications for government intervention in education *now*? In particular, are there *ethical* justifications?

If state schooling was an unequivocal success, the question might not arise, except for political economists and philosophers anxious to map out the limits of state power. But no-one can afford to be complacent about the shortcomings of state schooling. Its continuing difficulties prompt the question of why governments should be involved in education at all. It is this fundamental question which is explored in this monograph.[1]

The Failings of State Schooling

What are the failings of state schooling which motivate this inquiry? For a substantial minority of young people, state schooling fails them absolutely. They leave school without any qualifications, and apparently little else of benefit. An even larger number of young people – after 11 or more years of compulsory state schooling – is 'functionally' illiterate and innumerate – that is, unable to cope with the reading and numerical demands of everyday living. In Britain, for example, roughly 10 per cent of young people leave schools without any qualifications whatsoever, while 40 per cent of 21-year-olds *admit* to difficulties with writing and spelling, nearly 30 per cent difficulties with numeracy, and 20 per cent

---

[1] The focus in this paper will be mainly on primary and secondary education, up to compulsory school-leaving age. Similar considerations are likely to apply to tertiary (further or higher) education, although the issue of 'qualification inflation' (see Dore, 1976) may bring in an additional perspective. This will be discussed in a later publication.

difficulties with reading and writing (Central Statistical Office, 1995, p.58).[2]

Furthermore, for many young people, compulsory schooling cultivates little more than a culture of delinquency. The international study, *Pyschosocial Disorders in Young People*, shows how the 'crime rate increases swiftly to a peak in the teenage years between 15 and 17' (Rutter and Smith, 1995, pp.395-96), the years at the tail end of compulsory schooling; O'Keeffe (University of North London, 1994), in his study of English schools, found that over 30 per cent of students regularly or sometimes played truant from school; Lott (1987a, 1987b) showed that in the USA, even after controlling for factors such as urbanisation, parental income, and youth unemployment, as the proportion of children attending state schools increased, so there was an associated increase in juvenile delinquency rates.

State Schooling and Youth Alienation

Some have gone so far as to argue that compulsory schooling seems to be implicated in the growth of an alienating youth culture. Hargreaves observes:

'If one wanted to create a separate teenage culture, if one wanted to make adolescents feel cut-off from adult responsibilities, the best way would be to do as we now do: segregate them for most of their lives outside the family with those who happen to have been born in the same year' (Hargreaves, 1994, p.27).

Rutter and Smith (1995, p.801) suggest that it is precisely the growth of this 'isolated youth culture' that leads to the increase in youth alcoholism, drug dependency, suicide and depression, as well as crime.

Even considering those for whom state schooling is supposed to be a success, there arise many doubts about its efficacy. It is argued that young people are not being equipped with the skills and knowledge needed for 'employability' (Bierhoff and Prais, 1995, Industry in Education, 1996); they are ignorant and apathetic about the responsibilities of citizenship (Fogelman, 1991); they lack entrepreneurial talent

---

[2] Even these figures understate the problem: when given questions to answer, the same survey found that, for example, 90 per cent of 21-year-olds failed a test to work out discount prices of clothes in a sale, 67 per cent failed to work out the area of a carpet, and 77 per cent failed to be able to interpret a literary passage.

and economic understanding (Watts and Moran, 1984, Halil and Whitehead, 1990); and they are not adequately equipped to partake in learning throughout life (Ball, 1993, Ranson, 1994).

Finally, it is at least odd that, while other activities have been dramatically transformed over the last two or three decades by the information technology revolution, the technology of schooling remains resolutely fixed in the 19th century. Is one teacher to a class of 30 children (with only perfunctory access to computers) the most efficient and effective way of engaging in teaching and learning given the information technology revolution? This seems highly unlikely; more likely is that this is another instance of schooling failing to respond to changing opportunities and needs.

Many would go along with this summary of failures of state schooling, but would adopt one of two lines of defence of the principle of state intervention. *First*, they would either give voice to the 'British Rail Appeal',[3] that it is 'the wrong sort of' government intervention that is to blame – perhaps we have not had comprehensive enough comprehensives; or we should have eradicated the private schools; or we have pandered to left-wing teaching unions for too long, or whatever. Or, *second*, they might argue that, whatever the problems with state education, any market alternative would be even worse. The argument in this monograph is that both these responses are misguided.

State Intervention in Education

Some Definitions

Before setting out the structure of the paper, we need to be clear what is meant by government intervention in education, and by markets. Governments can intervene in education – as in any other area of welfare – in any of three ways: regulation, provision, and funding (Barr, 1993, p.80). Governments can regulate the supply side (for example, aiming to ensure

---

[3] Officials at British Rail once apologised to passengers for cancelled services involving brand new trains because 'the wrong sort of snow' had fallen, which the train manufacturer had apparently not designed the engines to encounter.

quality through a national curriculum and national testing), as well as demand (for instance, through compulsory schooling). Intervention in provision involves the state itself producing the goods and services (by building schools and employing teachers). Finally, state intervention in funding can be either 'direct' or 'indirect'. Direct funding entails government subsidy (or taxation) of the price of the good, wholly or in part ('free' schooling). Indirect funding comes through income transfers by the state, although these transfers can themselves either be tied to a certain end (for instance, via education vouchers) or untied (via general social security benefits, for example).

It is clear that in all current education systems, government intervenes in all three respects, and with direct, rather than indirect, funding. However, the various forms of intervention are separable and independent: just because government intervenes in one respect, does not mean it has to in the others. We can clarify the independence of these factors by looking to other areas of government intervention: the British government is seeking to fund the Channel Tunnel Rail Link through private finance (provision separate from funding); UK state regulation compels car drivers to wear seat belts, but there is no state funding or provision of these (regulation separate from funding and provision); finally, social security benefits are primarily to provide food and clothing for families, but there are no state food or clothing stores (funding separate from provision).

Without government intervention in any of these areas (except general regulation to provide the legal framework for contracts and the rule of law), there would be a pure 'market' in education. Lying between this extreme and the other of detailed state regulation, provision and finance, is an (infinite) variety of possibilities, all of which embody some features of markets and aspects of state control. We will find it useful in what follows to describe the situations where governments relinquish control in any of these areas as 'moves towards markets'. Where the balance of state intervention on all three fronts is reduced, we will often refer to the situation, in a rather rough and ready way, as a 'market', as is the current usage, although it must be remembered that such 'markets' embody many features of state intervention. We will also talk

14

of moves towards 'more authentic' markets, when the balance of state intervention is reduced still further.[4]

Structure of the Paper

For many, the response to the question of why states should be involved in education will be sheer incredulity that without state intervention, particularly in the areas of funding and provision, there would be any educational opportunities at all. State education is so all-pervasive that at first it seems hard to imagine what the alternative – markets in education – could be like.

However, we do have access to some of the possibilities of markets in education if, instead of focussing on children's education, we think of the education of adults. Even here, a word of caution is in order: for, it is possible that our education system so effectively stamps out the love of learning in young people that the educational market for adults is nowhere near as rich and diverse as it might otherwise be. That said, if I want to learn jazz piano, say, I can go to 'the educational market' and choose between the variety of means on offer, from cassettes, CD-ROMs and books, through college courses, to individual home tuition. Or if you want to learn how to keep fit, you have a similar range of choice from a diversity of possibilities – from joining a jogging pack, signing on with a gym, attending aerobics classes in a local church hall, buying a Jane Fonda cassette or video, or taking hints from general interest magazines. In *these* educational markets, there is real choice and real diversity.

But are these 'educational markets'? For they are not what most people mean by 'education'. Education is to do with young people and children, not 30-something jazz *aficionados* or couch potatoes. Education is to do with learning mathematics and geography and English, and the socialisation of children. Above all, education *takes place in schools*, and can it seriously be argued that there could be a market in schools?

---

[4] Readers might like to think of a three-dimensional space, with the axes representing government intervention in regulation, provision and finance. The origin would then be the 'pure market', and moves towards the origin from any point in the space would be moves towards a 'more authentic' market.

That is the first major concern that has to be addressed. This paper considers it in two ways. Chapter 2 conducts a thought experiment to explore what education without the state could look like. As the assumptions underlying this model depend in part upon some historical assumptions, I then turn to historical evidence concerning education without the state in Chapter 3. This provides an interesting case-study in its own right, of course, as it illustrates the possibilities and limitations of a genuine market in education. The argument in the first two chapters, then, can be seen as putting forward a quite radical 'market model' for education, with government having only very minimal rôles in *regulation* and *indirect funding* – the latter only for those too poor to cater for themselves – and none at all in *provision* of schooling.

Chapters 4 and 5 then explore possible objections to this model. A useful international literature has emerged in recent years criticising moves towards so-called 'markets' in education in Australia, New Zealand, South Africa, the United Kingdom, the United States, and elsewhere. These 'markets' typically permit some parental choice mechanisms, against a background of continued state intervention in provision and direct funding, together (usually) with strengthened central regulation. This critique is used here, suitably adapted where appropriate, to take into account conditions of more authentic markets, to probe the robustness of the market model. The most important of these objections to markets in education, concerning equality of opportunity, equity, democracy and the curriculum, and the information problem, are explored in Chapters 4 and 5. The upshot of this discussion is that the radical market model survives the critique.

Finally, in Chapter 6, tentative moves 'towards privatisation' of schooling are discussed. Some modest reforms are suggested which build on reforms introduced in England and Wales – similar to the other reforms mentioned above – to show how market incentives can be introduced and strengthened in a state schooling system to improve educational opportunities for all.

Markets are not popular amongst educationalists. The extensive literature suggests that they are perceived as undermining most of what educationalists hold dear. This paper suggests these fears are misguided. Moving towards more authentic markets will not undermine, but rather strengthen, the values and aspirations of concerned educators.

2 | What If....? A Thought Experiment on Markets and Education

Given the international ubiquity of state intervention in education, there are two ways of approaching the question of what education 'without the state' would be like. The first is to borrow the philosophical method of the 'thought experiment'. We imagine a world where most other factors about human nature, values and society are familiar, but bring in, in this case, the difference that governments are not involved in education. Can we imagine this world? The hope is that this process will illuminate our understanding of the aims of education, and what justified educational rôle for government there might be. Clearly, this method – a respectable part of any philosopher's repertoire – can be enhanced if we can model our thinking as closely as possible on any actual situation where states are, or were, not involved in education. Hence the second approach, taken up in Chapter 3, which explores the historical example of education in England and Wales prior to state intervention. Many of the assumptions made in this chapter will depend on the findings of that discussion. Others will become explicit as we proceed through the argument.

Rather than proceed on my thought experiment unaided, I build on the thought experiment conducted recently by Charles Murray, in his *In Pursuit: Of Happiness and Good Government* (1994), as a springboard for my own ideas.[1]

Murray's Thought Experiment

Murray's thought experiment starts with a community of parents, who

> 'for some reason find themselves without a school for their children and no way to get one except to set one up for themselves. The public [i.e. state] school system has disappeared – never mind why or how.' (Murray, 1994, p.182)

---

[1] West (1994a, Ch. 13) provides a powerful example of this type of thought experiment, one used as the motivation for Tooley, 1995a.

The parents are not rich nor poor, and they live in a town with others who are not parents. (He explores situations where parents are poor, etc., later, as we will do below.) *First*, he asks: 'Will they set up a school at all?', and because of historical evidence similar to that reviewed in the next chapter, concludes that they will:

> 'In a society where more education means more opportunity, parents of all classes left to their own devices have done whatever was necessary to educate their children. If our ... parents live in a free society, they will without doubt set up some sort of school.' (p.183)

Second, 'Who will be the teachers?'. He suggests that, although some will be attracted to teaching because of its intrinsic rewards, the financial rewards might not be great enough to staff the schools fully. So parents might have to lure teachers to the job with non-monetary rewards, including the respect given from parents and students alike, working autonomy, and the flexibility that a teaching career could offer. In any case, the conclusion is that the parents in his model 'have access to large numbers of people who would be willing and excellent teachers' (p.187). Without the state, Murray contends that educational opportunities will be provided in this community.

The historical evidence presented in the next chapter will strengthen Murray's conclusion that the parents in his model would be able to find and afford educational opportunities for their children. However, for most educationalists, there will be two main problems with his discussion; there is also a third problem, to which I return shortly. *First*, Murray assumes that parents who care about their children's education do in fact know what is best for their children and are able to select teachers who will teach accordingly and to an appropriate curriculum. However, this would be a big objection to markets in education raised by many educationists. In economic terms, it raises the issues concerning both efficiency and equity. For there will be fears that the system will be inefficient (if the parents do not have sufficient information to make these curriculum decisions); and it will be feared that the system will be inequitable (if the knowledge and access to this information is sensitive to, say, socio-economic status). In terms more familiar in current educational debates, it raises

18

the very important issue of government regulation of the curriculum, and of providing information to parents through testing, league tables, and so on. These concerns will be put aside for now, to be addressed in Chapter 5 (hence any conclusions about markets here will be tentative in lieu of this discussion).

Second, the main reaction to Murray's model as described so far may well be 'so what?'. Only the easiest case has been examined, and it is crucially the issues of the curriculum and information, and what would happen to the children of less concerned or poorer families, that will be of concern to those who oppose markets.

If this is the viewpoint of some readers, then something important has been conceded: for not-poor and concerned parents, the suggestion is that there is no rôle for state funding or provision of schooling, and only, perhaps (depending on our later discussion), a role for the state in regulation of the curriculum and providing information. We will return to this later. But first, in thought experiment mode, let us move to scenarios where parents are not all educationally concerned and some are poor, where some young people do not want the good things education offers, and where there are larger and more diverse communities. Will these situations bring out the deficiencies of markets?

Modifications to the Model

It is useful to consider three types of situations, breaking away gradually from Murray's model. *First*, a community identical to Murray's, of 'educationally concerned' parents, except that it is not quite wealthy enough, would find it something of a struggle financially, to provide the schooling he envisages. To keep things simple, all the families have roughly the same amount of (inadequate) income. *Second*, a mixed setting where Murray's better-off community also has some much poorer parents as members, who would find it absolutely impossible to afford schooling. Some of these will be 'educationally concerned', others not. *Third*, we will explore what happens to the model when there are poor communities completely separate from wealthier communities.

The first modification has Murray's community as he described it, but now unable to afford the schooling that it desires. The parents – still 'educationally concerned', by

19

assumption – find that their educational expectations exceed the resources they have available for schooling. What will they do? Will they shrug and give up on educational provision for their children? That seems highly unlikely. If schooling is too expensive, the concerned parents will explore alternatives. Some of the parents will begin to think about the school budget, looking for ways to cut costs – with the constraint, because they are concerned parents, that their children's education cannot be compromised.

First, they look at the way teaching is conducted in the too-expensive model of schooling elsewhere, and puzzle over whether it is the most efficient and effective method of educating youngsters. They look at the traditional model, with one teacher and 30-odd children, and one old computer shared with several classes, and wonder about the educational sense of this arrangement. After all, one parent says, this was all very well in our day, but that was before the days of cheap information technology – which, someone else ruefully observes, has cut many of their own working hours. Every other business is using information technology to cut costs, why not teaching? Someone else points out that such technology is unlikely to jeopardise their children's education, because there are excellent learning packages available which can enable children to learn all the traditional subjects, and more, at their own pace. It seems that a different combination of teachers, assistant teachers and information technology might be cheaper as well as more appropriate for effective teaching and learning.

The parents do some calculations. Instead of one teacher for 30 students, why not have one teacher for 60 students, with technology substituted for the absent teacher? For each teacher lost, £25,000 per year (a typical teacher's salary) would be saved. Over a four-year period, this £100,000 would purchase 30 multimedia systems and software (at £1,000 each), and one teaching assistant (at £10,000 per year) and still leave £30,000 in savings! This would be a very sensible way of attempting to save money. Under this new arrangement, one teacher could still teach a class of 30, as in other, wealthier schools, while the other 30 children got on with their own work on the computers, supervised by the teaching assistant.

Other models are proposed, with different variations on the same theme, bringing in television, video and radio, as well as the computers and CD-ROMs. All produce substantial savings – perhaps, even by this measure alone, the financial crisis could be averted. No-one could argue that there would inevitably be a decline in educational standards as a result.

Asking Different Questions

But suppose that even these measures could not solve the problem. Are there any other ways the parents could save costs without putting the education of their children at risk? They puzzle over this, and begin to ask some fundamental questions. What is the school for? What is education? The parents bring employers, community and religious leaders, and young people too, into their discussions.

The parents first. Above all they want their children to grow up to be independent and responsible persons, able to find employment and provide for themselves; they want their children to be happy and able to enjoy the good things in life; many want them to be responsible citizens, aware of the wider needs of the community. The employers brought into the discussion say they want 'employable' youngsters, pointing to qualities such as good manners, punctuality, diligence, and so on, as well as basic literacy and numeracy and computing skills. A few will point to more specialised skills that they seek, such as advanced mathematics or technical drawing. The young people have their say. They want to know what they are studying for, and to feel it is relevant to their situation, and to the wider community. Many too say that they want adult rôle models, and to be able to discover what possibilities there are in adult life.

Now that the community is exploring these issue, it seems that the crisis of not being able to afford schooling has led them to think through the functions of their school. It soon becomes obvious that many of the qualities, skills and knowledge that it had previously been assumed only schools could provide could better be developed in the community itself. Personal qualities of perseverance, responsibility, citizenship, getting on with people, and problem solving, for example, seem particularly suited to being developed through voluntary service in the community, by looking after the sick, elderly or handicapped. Moreover, these give young people a genuine sense that they are doing something worthwhile. On vocational training, the community starts to view the

21

experience elsewhere of allocating this to the school with some incredulity. Is this not far better obtained in various workplaces themselves? Indeed, some of the students pipe up at this point, saying that their friends elsewhere have always said teachers were not convincing in the rôle of introducing young people to the world of work, not having themselves experienced any world of work outside the school!

Similarly, other activities seem better moved away from the school. For sport, instead of relying on the rather expensive services of the Physical Education teacher, why not utilise the many retired, unemployed or partially employed men and women in the community who would like nothing more than organising games and events for young people? Several young people themselves point out that they would be very happy helping out with younger children. Music and art are similarly catered for. The need for these particular expensive teachers is becoming far less significant, the community itself growing far more confident and vibrant in the rôle it is assuming.

Moreover, even in richer communities elsewhere, it is pointed out that there are costs related to youth crime: the parents begin to see now the way in which schools 'ghettoise' youth, separating them from the community and taking them away from adult rôle models. Perhaps if their own young people are reintegrated into the community in the ways envisaged, then these costs could also be avoided or reduced?

However, by this stage, some in the community are becoming rather concerned that the situation seems rather anarchic: above all, they admit, one of the functions of the school had been to supervise children while adults were at work, or simply to get children out of the house. It is all very well having all these opportunities available in the community, but how do they know that young people will be engaged in doing them? So it is suggested that the school building becomes a sort of 'clearing house', where young people sign on and off, where the rota of activities is organised, where the teaching and learning of some subjects takes place, and where some form of check on students keeping to their outside commitments is conducted.

Having started to think radically in this way, the community now begins to see further ways of saving money: the school has quite extensive sports fields which are now no longer required, as the local town sports fields are now more than adequate. Perhaps these could be sold as building land, and the money used to reduce schooling costs further? Or some of the old technology classrooms are no longer needed, as students have hands-on experience in local companies now: perhaps these can be leased to the local hotel wishing to expand its conference facilities? But enough: the town is in a recession, and none of these ideas can get off the ground this year; most importantly, with all the measures so far suggested, the financial crisis is already solved. With the cost-cutting measures introduced, all can afford the schooling they desire for their children.

By 'asking different questions', as Murray would put it, the community has solved its educational funding crisis. But even if, in this particular community, the parents had not been able to do this lateral thinking, it would not matter too much, as long as elsewhere some educational entrepreneurs (or philosophers!) were exploring these ideas in some similar community. For then there would be examples of coping with such a crisis to follow, and all our community would have to do would be to imitate, rather than initiate.

This brings me to my *third* objection to Murray's model: for *even if the school system was actually functioning rather well*, with everyone able to afford it, anyone could begin to think along the lines outlined above, and come up with ideas on how to improve the system, on how to make it run as effectively but at a cheaper price. Murray was being rather unimaginative in his model. He accepted the traditional picture of the traditional school, with a traditional pupil-teacher ratio, and did not consider the possibility of an educational entrepreneur arriving or emerging in the community. He forgot that he was describing a market, where entrepreneurs can seek out opportunities, weigh up possibilities, and have incentives to act on their visions. So there would be nothing to stop the situation described here taking place in the community of richer folk, transforming schooling in ways that were not readily apparent to Murray.

The purpose of this thought experiment was to explore the need for state intervention in education. What I have suggested is that, for concerned and not-poor parents, in our model there is no need for the state to be involved at all (apart from the issue of the curriculum, which we explore below, in Chapter 5). But even for those not so wealthy but concerned families, or families going through hard times, there still might not be any need for the state to intervene, precisely because there seem to be many ways in which schooling can be improved or standards maintained while simultaneously cutting costs.

Introducing Inequality

The model needs further modification. We have seen what happens when there is a community of less wealthy people all on more or less the same income; what happens when inequalities of income are introduced into the picture? Moreover, what happens when there are unconcerned families, or recalcitrant children?

Consider first that Murray's community has some proportion too poor to pay for their children's educational opportunities, although they are still educationally concerned. It has turned out that many of the community's educationally valuable activities do not require money (the conflation of schooling and education has been broken), so it would seem likely that all can take part in them, poor or not. These include community service, vocational work experience, perhaps some sports, music and drama, and so on. Moreover, having some people unable to afford the whole package of educational opportunities provides exactly the incentive for entrepreneurs to address the issue. With some imaginative thinking along the lines above, it would not necessarily be the case that just because people were poorer, they could not afford adequate opportunities. With imagination, lack of resources could result in existing resources being used better.

But suppose that none of these possibilities is available, or that there remain some people still too poor to take advantage of these options. If the community neglects the children of the poor, then it runs the risk of bearing 'negative externalities'[2] – if, say, the children become unemployed, and hence unproductive, or turn to crime, as the result of lack of educational opportunities. Similarly, if the community were to

---

[2] Formally, an external effect, or externality, arises when one individual imposes costs (negative externalities) or benefits (positive externalities) on another, for which no compensation or payment or insufficient compensation or payment between the individuals takes place.

see to the educational provision of the poor, then there could be 'positive externalities', in the form of increased productivity, or of increased social cohesion, or simply the pleasures of more well-educated young people with whom to interact. So community members would be well-advised, *in their own self-interest*, to find additional funds for these poorer members, to subsidise those educational opportunities that are missing. It might not even mean finding *additional* funds, of course. For the marginal cost of bringing in a couple of extra students into the school, or using the computers, could be zero, or very close to zero.

Finally, bringing in altruism provides a completely new dimension, of course. It may be that in the community, people want to provide for poorer members out of simple generosity, and will offer formal or informal bursaries to them. So in a mixed richer and poorer community, provided the poor do not overwhelm the more wealthy members, there seems no need to override the market to provide educational opportunities for all (with the usual caveat that we do not know as yet about the curriculum). The life of the community can ensure this, in tandem with the incentives provided by self-interest and altruism.[3]

Next, consider the case where parents are not interested in the education of their children, or the children are not themselves interested. Again, so long as these parents do not overwhelm the community, then a similar solution to the above might arise. Because of the interest in avoiding negative externalities, the rest of the community is likely to put pressure on the recalcitrant parents, or go over the heads of the parents and offer opportunities to the children themselves. But what if none of this works? Suppose there is a minority determined to resist educational opportunities for their children (or, by the children, for themselves). Perhaps parents want their children to work for them, to bring in income. Perhaps they are abusive of them. Here there would seem to be the first rôle for the state: to show this it is necessary to step back from the thought experiment and bring in an additional assumption.

---

[3] If the reader is not convinced by this argument, then he or she can substitute the conclusion arrived at below when we consider wholly poor communities, of some state subsidies, to resolve this situation.

There is a long tradition of liberal thought which points to the need for governments to invoke a 'protection of minors' principle. Families do not have absolute power over their children; it can be incorporated into the 'constitution of liberty' that the state can intervene if it is discovered that a child is being abused in these ways. That is the line taken in two seminal works exploring the possibilities of markets in education, by Peacock and Wiseman (1964) and West ([1965], 1994a).

E.G. West points out that even the most ardent 19th-century supporters of *laissez-faire* made an exception to the 'general principle of freedom of contract' when defenceless children were at risk, and proposes some minimal state regulation to ensure that all do have a minimum standard of education available (West [1965], 1994a, p.290). Alan Peacock and Jack Wiseman take the line that government has a responsibility to 'ensure universal education up to some minimum level' (Peacock and Wiseman, 1964, p.27).[4] But notice that even with this assumption, it does not necessarily mean the whole gamut of state intervention to ensure universal education: in the communities we have discussed thus far, the state has not needed do *anything* to ensure this universal provision. It is only now that there is a case for it to intervene.

So if all else fails in the community, there may well be a need to appeal to the state to intervene to compel those parents to allow their children to partake of the educational opportunities available. There does seem to be a reasonable argument that some of these children will be harmed by their parents' neglect. Notice that this does not necessarily mean, in these communities, that the state would also need to fund

---

[4] Notice there are differences between these two accounts. Peacock and Wiseman do suggest that universal compulsion and funding would probably be necessary in order to meet this responsibility; West, however, thinks that only selective compulsion and funding is needed. We side with the latter viewpoint, partly because this seems to be where our thought experiment is taking us, but also because it seems likely that Peacock and Wiseman would have changed their view on this, had they been aware of West's work (they published before him). West's argument is reviewed in the next chapter. Others have changed their mind on this crucial issue, including the influential Milton Friedman, who backtracked on his ideas of the need for univeral compulsion after having read West (see Friedman and Friedman, 1980, p.162 and fn.15).

these opportunities. The community is likely to be able to do that for itself, as outlined above. All it needs is for the state to compel selectively.[5]

Coercion of this sort would be far less threatening than it might appear. Children could be selectively compelled for a while to partake of educational opportunities offered by their local community, and if this is clearly not effective, or the children are too disruptive, then the compulsion would be lifted. But note that many of the reasons why children are disruptive or resist educational opportunities will be removed. They will not be put into the technologically primitive situation of one teacher and 30 children for all their time in school. They will have a wealth of educational opportunities available outside the school setting. The resistance to *schooling* so apparent in many societies may not be resistance to *education* more broadly conceived. Children are not being compelled to be in custody, but only to get a sense of the educational opportunities that are available. So it may well be that only a small amount of compulsion – a pump-priming exercise – would do the job.

Note the key point here: there is a need for *selective* compulsion only. That is, there is a separate solution for those educationally irresponsible parents. Both of the above mentioned key works agree on this: Peacock and Wiseman note that

> 'it is unsatisfactory in principle to base general principles upon the special needs of a minority ... the existence of some "problem families" is [not] an argument for general limitations of the rights and responsibilities of parents for their children' (Peacock and Wiseman, 1964, p.19).

West draws a parallel with the approach to the protection of children from physical neglect – where the state

> 'has means to see to it that no family is without the purchasing power necessary to feed and clothe a child to a certain standard ... health visitors .. can appeal to Child Abuse Laws to instigate what amounts to legal compulsion of the parents' (West [1965], 1994a, p.253).

---

[5] It is no argument to say that if goverment compels, then it should also fund: as we noted earlier, seat-belts are compulsory, but are not state-funded.

Next, what of those communities which have an overwhelming majority of poor people, or those with an overwhelming majority of educationally irresponsible parents or young people? At first it might be thought that we could apply all the above arguments to the case of the poor communities too. It probably is in the interests of neighbouring communities to be concerned with the poorer communities since the young people in them might pose a threat later on. Of course, there is also the sense of common humanity, altruism, which will make other communities concerned for the well-being of these children (and children will always be an easy source of charity, because there will always be the notion that it definitely is not 'their fault': children will always be the 'deserving' poor). But here there is a problem.

While we have not stretched the bounds of the imagination in suggesting that the communities discussed earlier would be able to find the resources (or initiatives to save resources) for *their own* poorer members, it might well be that in this new situation, the extra resources could not be found, perhaps because the pull of self-interest and altruism are not as strong for these neighbouring communities. In any case, part of the beauty of the earlier examples was that the marginal costs of allowing the poor into educational opportunities were likely to be zero or near zero. That is not so any more. At least travel costs would have to be paid to bring the poor to the facilities, and there might well be disincentives to have them in, because of uncertainty about their community ethos, and fears that they would be disruptive in some ways.

Perhaps one way around this would be for a much wider appeal for resources to help this poorer community, an appeal to which regional, national or even international philanthropic or commercial sources might respond. But suppose that people do not respond to the appeal, or do not respond with enough resources. Or suppose that no-one notices the plight of the community in the first place, or is prepared to advertise its need. Then what? Again, there seems to be a case for that instrument of last resort, the state, to have enshrined in its constitution that it can enter to ensure the educational needs of these communities are fully met. Notice that its rôle initially might simply be to do the advertising of need, to act as a sorting house, matching potential funders to needy communities. Then if, after some period (say, six months) sufficient funds had been found, the state could be permitted to step in with resources too.[6] It is only resources which are required. With money, by hypothesis, these communities will now look for educational opportunities, and will be the same as the earlier mentioned communities.

Finally, what about those educationally irresponsible communities? Again, exactly as in the example above, it seems likely that, after other channels are exhausted, the state might be needed as a funder and compeller of last resort.

Minimal State Intervention

What we have arrived at is as follows. Education and training are desirable in society. Schooling as we know it now is not necessarily the best way to provide them. If we were to start from scratch, a community or society might decide that some aspects of the educational needs of society are best met through specialised institutions, but that others are not. What this suggests is that, if educational institutions had been allowed to evolve, rather than being pushed into one model by governments, we might see a completely different situation now from that which has been brought about, for example, by government intervention in England and Wales over the last 120 or so years.

However, the thought experiment clearly points to the need for two sorts of government intervention to ensure that all have educational opportunities. *First*, government needs to fund selectively those too poor to avail themselves of existing opportunities. *Second*, it needs to compel selectively those who refuse to avail themselves of these opportunities. In other words, education has emerged from this discussion as a good, in some respects, very similar to food or clothing: for those goods, we say that government is only permitted a 'safety net' rôle in giving funds to poor parents and protecting children from abuse, by selective compulsion of negligent parents; this protection-of-minors principle does not require government provision or special regulation, nor does it require universal funding and compulsion.

---

[6] I borrow this method from the actual provision which was put forward in the 1870 Forster Act – more details of which follow in the next chapter.

No doubt many objections to the model will have occurred to readers. Perhaps the major issue arising from the discussion would be that of the curriculum and the information problem: these emerged as key objections to Murray's original model. Clearly the problem of the curriculum also arises when we consider the required minimum level of education which the state should ensure. The issue of equality or equity will also loom large to many readers. These issues are explored in depth in Chapters 4 and 5. But first, it will be apparent that the model described above depends upon there being a majority of parents of children who would be concerned with their children's education, and upon that majority being able to find the necessary funds. If these assumptions were not fulfilled, the whole model would collapse.

How did I feel able to make these rather optimistic assumptions in the thought experiment? They are based in part on the historical evidence of education without the state in England and Wales which is described in the next chapter.

3 | The Secret History of Education Without the State

There is a 'Far Side' cartoon by Gary Larson which shows an ordinary family in an ordinary living room, with parent, children and dog all paying rapt attention to ... an empty wall. The caption reads 'In the days before television ...'. Many people believe that, in the days before state schooling in Britain, there was a similar lacuna; that people idly sat around, waiting for the state to step in and fill the gap in their lives. Satisfying though this picture may be to those who favour government intervention in education, it does not appear to tally with the historical evidence. For E.G. West ([1965], 1994a) has argued that, before the state became involved in education in England and Wales in 1870,[1] the great majority of young people was in schooling, that literacy and numeracy rates were very high, and parents provided the greatest proportion of school fees. A similar phenomenon occurred in America before government involvement in education there (Richman, 1994, West, 1994a) and in Scotland (High and Ellig, 1992).

First, it is particularly important to review this evidence, partly because of the assumption made in Chapter 2, but also because the evidence shows a rare example of a practising market in education. *Second*, the evidence depends to a large degree on the seminal work of E.G. West; but West has received a great deal of criticism – indeed, notoriety – for these views. In certain circles, when West's account is mentioned, one is greeted with a certain weariness, and the suggestion that the ideas have all long been discredited. Wary of the danger of simply latching on to the story that offers most support to my argument, my methodology has been to take West's argument and then subject it to some of its sternest criticism in the literature. Moreover, I have used two historians against West whom West himself has not

---

[1] From the 1830s there was a very limited amount of government grants and some inspection.

31

challenged[2] – the suggestion by some being that their criticisms are unassailable. We can note in passing that it is not just the 'Right' that is inspired by West's argument; from the 'Left' we also have Johnson arguing that:

> 'One of the most interesting developments in working-class history has been the rediscovery of popular educational traditions, the springs of action of which owed little to philanthropic, ecclesiastical or state provision.' (Johnson, 1979, p.75)

He cites West as one of the sources of this revisionism.

In the next sections, the arguments about the quantity of schooling, the quality of schooling and the issue of the need for compulsion, are reviewed, to attempt to ascertain how justified the assault on West is.

Quantity of Schooling

West's argument is that, prior to the major state involvement in education through the 1870 Forster Act, school attendance rates and literacy rates were high. As regards literacy, West *first* notes the substantial circumstantial evidence, that until 1833 the action of the state was one of deliberate hindrance of individual efforts towards literacy (West, 1994a, p.158). Steam printing was introduced in the 1830s and caused reductions in the price of newspapers, which began to increase their sales, despite restrictive taxes: 'That a mass newspaper-reading public was already in existence well before 1870 is now firmly acknowledged by specialist writers' (p.159).

Second, he reviews statistical evidence, including records of educational qualifications of criminals, records of workhouse children, workplace literacy returns, and number of people signing the marriage register. From these various sources, he concludes that '93 per cent of school leavers were already literate when the 1870 board schools first began to operate' (p.167). As regards schooling, West uses a variety of widely available statistics, including the report of the Newcastle Commission on Popular Education, published in 1861. Its results showed that 95·5 per cent of children were in school for up to six years. The remaining 4·5 per cent, he argues, could

---

2   For an example of the historical debate in the literature, see Kiesling (1983) and West (1983).

be accounted for by sick children, children educated at home, and also perhaps an error in estimation (p.177). Moreover, on the funding of the educational opportunities, we find that even in the minority of schools in receipt of some state funding, two-thirds of funding came from non-state sources, including parents' contributions to fees, and Church and philanthropic funds (West, 1983, p.427). Even here the *biggest* part of the school fees was provided by parents (p.427).

A first disagreement with West seems apparent from the architect of the 1870 Act himself. For when Forster introduced his Education Bill of 1870 into parliament, he made no reference to the Newcastle Commission's findings, but relied on evidence from a small-scale survey conducted by two inspectors in 1869 over a period of a few months in four industrial towns, Liverpool, Manchester, Leeds and Birmingham (p.180). In Liverpool, for example, he argued that, out of an estimated 80,000 children of school age,

> '20,000 of them attend no school whatever, while at least another 20,000 attend schools where they get an education not worth having' (quoted on p.181).

At first glance this seems a major discrepancy. However, as was pointed out later in the parliamentary debates, it arises because of the definition of 'school age'. The Newcastle Commission had discovered that a typical child was at school for 5·7 years. Forster had assumed that the school age population was of children between the ages of 5 and 13 – that is, an eight-year schooling period. Even if we assume that the school-age period had increased from 5·7 to 6 years by the time of Forster's survey, then, instead of his estimated 80,000 children of school age, we are likely to find a reduced figure of 60,000 (that is, three-quarters of 80,000). This was exactly the figure that Forster's survey found in school! The fallacy that Forster committed would be rather like defining the proper school-leaving age in England today as 20 years, and then claiming that, say, 25 per cent of 'school-age' children were not in school at all.

Comparative Data

Moving to more recent disputes about West's interpretation of history, one widely quoted source of dissent comes from the educational historian Andy Green. He states that West 'has attempted to rehabilitate the reputation of English educational *laissez-faire*, arguing that reformers ... exaggerated English deficiencies. However, comparative data, which West largely ignores, vindicates the deficiency verdict, *at least in terms of the relative position of English education*' (Green, 1990, p.11, emphasis added).

That is, Green suggests that the main argument against the English system is that it was failing to achieve the same levels of enrolment and literacy as the heavily interventionist European states. However, when he reviews the evidence, it transpires that even according to him, England's relative position in the mid-19th century was *better than France's* as regards the percentage of the population receiving schooling (p.15), and with regard to adult literacy (p.25). Green neither disputes that there was a widespread 'national network' of schools in Victorian England and Wales without the state (p.8), nor does he dispute that this was more effective than the French centralised state educational system. It does not seem that his challenge to West is as substantial as he suggests. Other historians concur: W.B. Stephens notes that in the period 1850-90, 'the proportion of literate persons in England' was higher than in France, although lower than in Germany (Stephens, 1987, p.16).

Stephens is another important historian who has been strongly critical of West's position. *First*, he thinks that West has taken the Newcastle Commission's conclusions too literally. He says that their estimate of time spent in school was probably on the optimistic side:

'At all events this time probably included years spent as toddlers from three years of age upwards, and anyway, being an average, varied greatly from place to place, and was in practice reduced by irregular attendance.' (Stephens, 1987, p.52)

Now, even if Stephens is correct in this observation, it is clear that he is not undermining the basic claim of West. He is haggling over the specific percentage of children in schooling, or suggesting some geographical variations, not disputing West's fundamental claim that, with only very minimal state interference, schooling rates were very high. It is crucial to recall that this was in an age of great poverty. Perhaps the most important way to respond to this criticism for the purposes at hand, is to ask to what extent any geographical shortcomings in schooling provision or irregular attendance were the result of this poverty. This is addressed below, when we consider the need for compulsion.

The educational reformer and philosopher, John Stuart Mill, writing in 1834, would have concurred with our conclusion:

'As far, therefore, as *quantity* of teaching is concerned, the education of our people is, or will speedily be, amply provided for.'

However, he continues:

'It is the *quality* which so grievously demands the amending hand of government. And this is the demand which is principally in danger of being obstructed by popular apathy and ignorance' (quoted in Garforth, 1980, p.114).

This is crucial. Even if it is conceded that there was enough quantity of schooling, as I suggest West's critics would largely agree, this is still a long shot from saying that the schooling was of an 'adequate' quality without the state. What can be said about the quality of schooling in 19th-century England and Wales?

Quality of Schooling

It is worth remarking that with state involvement, the quality issue is not necessarily solved. For example, Green himself points out that, just because a state was heavily involved in education:

'this does not mean that what [was] taught was necessarily desirable from all points of view, and indeed, the kinds of knowledge and attitudes that were transmitted by the most efficient systems, notably in Prussia, often reflected most illiberal and doctrinaire purposes on the part of the state, and consequently engendered great suspicion amongst those with more democratic leanings.' (Green, 1990, p.8)

Similarly, there is Mill's well-known warning that:

'A general State education is a mere contrivance for moulding people to be exactly like one another. ... in proportion as it is efficient and successful, it establishes a despotism over the mind, leading by natural tendency to one over the body.' (Mill [1859], 1972, p.175)

So *with* the state controlling curriculum and teaching, there are clear problems concerning educational quality. But what about without?

The educational reformers of the 19th century were adamant that the quality of schooling needed to be improved, and could be improved only with state action. Critics of West's position have agreed with this. For example, Stephens notes:

> 'With the advent of government funding and inspection, followed by the introduction into public schools of pupil teachers, increasing numbers of trained teachers, better buildings and equipment, more generous provision of books and so on, the benefit of a sound curriculum and teaching methods, and the pressure for regular attendance, standards in inspected public schools, particularly from the 1850s, *must certainly have outstripped* those of schools reliant on local funding and school pence and under less external pressure.' (Stephens, 1987, p.25, emphasis added)

That is, the intervention of government had the effect of improving the quality of schooling, which would not otherwise have occurred. Is this true? *First*, it is not correct that these 'improvements' could have come about only through state intervention. Some of them were simply the result of more funds (buildings, equipment, books), and more funds could have come from other sources besides the state – from voluntary contributions, charities, or simply the improved wealth over time of the people buying schooling. Moreover, Stephens cannot mean that 'the pressure for regular attendance' was state-induced, because schooling did not become compulsory for some years after the period he is surveying. So this must have been something that happened irrespective of state involvement.

Note also that the type of state intervention he is referring to is minimal. These 'public schools' he is describing are simply publicly-inspected schools, with some small government subsidy. They are not what would be termed 'publicly provided' today. So even if Stephens is correct, and these were of much higher quality than the non-inspected schools, this would be an argument only for inspection and very small subsidy – intervention more in line with our thought experiment 'market model' and not an argument for state provision or funding in general.

36

Second, how can we be sure that the 'improvements' he describes did lead to higher standards? It is a common assumption today that better buildings, resources, trained teachers, and so on do lead to higher quality – but in recent years, researchers have tried to look for correlation between these variables and quality of education and found the connection uncertain at best, with other factors of far greater significance (see, for example, Chubb and Moe, 1990, Mortimore, 1995, Reynolds, 1982, Rutter *et al.*, 1979). As far as the situation in the 19th century is concerned, there may be other factors which undermine Stephens's conclusions.

Rote Learning for Teachers

Concerning trained teachers, West points out that teacher training at the time consisted overwhelmingly of rote learning and that it

'seems at least arguable that the communication of adults from varied occupations might, on average, have been more useful and inspiring to children in school rooms than parroting of English Literature before young school teachers who, in their own lives, had had little time to do anything else' (West, 1994a, p.210).

Johnson notes the preponderance of politically radical teachers in the uninspected schools:

'Teaching was indeed an obvious resource for an intelligent, self-educated man or woman especially if he or she had already fallen foul of employers or other authorities.' (Johnson, 1979, p.81)

Doubts must also be cast on Stephens's suggestion that government inspection also led to higher quality of education: the inspectors' early official concept of educational efficiency meant 'a schooling which scored high marks in divinity and morality' (West, 1994a, p.104). Indeed, some schools were deemed worthless precisely because of failure in moral and religious training. But it is likely that many parents felt that these aspects of education were being largely catered for in the family and in the Sunday Schools – 'on week-days families were demanding education in more "practical" matters' (p.91), such as reading, writing and arithmetic. Moreover, it must be noted that inspectors making these criticisms are known to have had particular biases. For example, H.S. Tremenheere, in the early 1850s, noted that the people's education enabled

37

them to read 'seditious literature without having the moral or intellectual strength to discern its falseness' (quoted by Stephens, 1987, p.133). This was literature which was 'exaggerating the principle of equality before God and the law', and encouraging workers to be antagonistic towards their employers (p.133). With prejudices like these, it may well be that the inspector's reports were not as valuable as Stephens elsewhere suggests, nor as likely to lead to improved quality of educational experiences.

Again, the assumption that better buildings were likely to have led to educational improvements may also be far-fetched. It too may have had no impact at all on children – indeed, it may well have meant schooling in large, cold, regimented, factory-like surroundings, rather than the cosy schoolroom of the dame school, and may have been detrimental to educational purposes (see Gardner, 1984).

Stephens does give some additional evidence to support his claims, but none of it seems substantial. He says that the uninspected schools were

'certainly less efficient than the inspected schools. It was reckoned that in the uninspected schools of Birmingham less than a quarter of pupils would have passed the appropriate examination under the Revised Code' (Stephens, 1987, p.149).

But this raises more questions than it answers. How many would have passed in the inspected schools? How was the previous figure obtained, if the schools were not inspected? Were the inspected schools better because of better training of teachers, etc., or was there some other reason? We are left in the dark about answers to all these important questions.

Some schools were run 'cheaply with uncertified teachers and poor equipment; they were thus unable to obtain government grants and a bad situation was compounded' (p.204). But why does this say that the quality of schooling was low? No evidence is given that these certified teachers really were any better. One particularly revealing piece of evidence comes from a report of the inspectorate from Monmouthshire, which showed that 'educational progress since 1853' had been marked, but then points out that this cannot have been the case, because of the low number of certified teachers and schools given grants.

Green is also ready to challenge West on the quality of schooling in 19th-century England and Wales. He argues that even the quality of *post-elementary* schooling for the middle-classes was inferior to that found in continental Europe. He arrives at this conclusion by noting that there were only 100 secondary schools in England and Wales that even aspired to the standards of the German *Gymnasien*; 'and one may doubt whether any of these matched the latter's academic standards' (Green, 1990, p.17). But even if this figure of 100 is correct, then this is to be compared with 139 *Gymnasien* (p.16) – more, true, but not considerably so. Moreover, in France, there were only 77 *lycées*.

But how is his figure of 100 obtained? He notes that there were in total, according to the Taunton Commission of 1868, nine public schools, 46 boarding schools and 209 endowed grammar schools, plus a 'dense outgrowth of "lesser" private schools' (p.17). As the Commissioners found most of the lesser private schools 'unspeakably bad', and the endowed grammar schools generally 'very unsatisfactory' and 'chaotic' (p.17), Green wants to omit most of these from his calculations. For reasons already given, we are wary of these commissioners' reports. But let us go along with Green's acceptance of them, to see what follows. For even he accepts that 70 of the grammar schools sent children to university, which suggests that these at least cannot have been that bad. So even taking these 70, and adding them to the 46 and nine upper-class élitist schools, then we actually have not 100 but 125 schools – which is much closer to the German figure, and nearly twice as high as that in France. But note that, while he has doubted the quality of the majority of the English schools, he has assumed that *all* of the continental schools were of a high standard. How is he justified in making such an assumption? Perhaps if there had been similar Commissions set up in Prussia and France, they too would have found some at least of those schools below standard? It seems that Green's evidence does not lead to the conclusion that the quality of education without the state in England and Wales was necessarily so bad after all, given the relative poverty of the period.

One final complaint of the 19th-century reformers must be mentioned: in the 1830s the Manchester Statistical Society complained that pupil-teacher ratios were too high. The figure they found was 26·8 pupils per teacher. In 1967 there were 29·7 pupils per teacher in English primary schools (West, 1970, p.90). In 1994/95 it was 22·2!

We conclude that, given the poverty of the period, the quality of education in the market may not have been as bad as was suggested by contemporary observers, and reinforced by those modern historians who seek to challenge West. Given an increase in the wealth of the nation, all the improvements noted by the historians could have occurred anyway without state intervention.

Extended Education Outside Schools

Remember too that the discussion is about the quality of *schooling*, and not 'education' more generally. Education elsewhere in children's lives is not taken into account in many of the above criticisms. In homes, communities, churches, etc., there may have been extensive educational opportunities, which may well have been vastly superior to those received by children in schools late this century. For example, Johnson comments on one undervalued 'popular educational resource: the working-class family itself' (Johnson, 1979, p.75), where families must be understood in the extended sense of fathers, mothers, uncles and grandparents (pp.80ff). He notes that part of the tradition of working-class 'radical education' was a critique of all forms of provided education, including opposition to a centralised state system (p.76) and an emphasis on 'men and women as educators of their own children' (p.77). In addition, he notes the educational resources of

> 'neighbourhood and even place of work, whether within the household or outside of it, the acquisition of literacy from mothers of fathers, the use of the knowledgeable friend or neighbour, or the "scholar" in neighbouring town or village, the work-place discussion and formal and informal apprenticeships, the extensive network of private schools and, in many cases, the local Sunday schools, most un-school-like of the new devices, excellently adapted to working-class needs ... communal reading and discussion groups, the facilities for newspapers in pub, coffee house or reading room, the broader cultural politics of Chartist or Owenite branch-life, the institution of the travelling lecturer. ... and, above all, the radical press, the most successful radical invention and an extremely flexible (and therefore ubiquitous) educational reform... best thought of as a series of educational networks' (p.80).

The message from this is that schooling is not the same as education, and a broader perspective must be used to assess the full quality of educational experiences of children in the 19th century.

Thus far in this historical survey, it can be concluded that West's position seems to emerge relatively unscathed. It is likely that the remaining problems of insufficient quantity or poor quality of schooling could have been solved by increased wealth, as West notes, rather than state intervention. The problem was low income, not a low importance attached to schooling or education more generally. This historical survey seems to provide support to the assumption in the thought experiment of Chapter 2 about the numbers of families who would be educationally 'concerned', and wealthy enough to afford educational opportunities.

However, it is commonly held that not only did the state need to become involved in the funding of schooling from 1870, but that an essential part of its later intervention was also to make schooling compulsory. Only in this way could adequate educational opportunities be provided for all. Does the historical evidence support this part of the accepted wisdom?

Compulsory Schooling

Stephens notes:

> 'Since schooling generally was not free and did not begin to become compulsory until the 1870s, the rising school attendance figures over the two generations before that must reflect a growing demand from working-class parents for formal schooling, however minimal' (Stephens, 1987, pp.48-49).

The 'however minimal' seems rather grudging: in fact, while the real growth in income over the period 1801-71 was just over 1 per cent a year, the average annual growth rate of school pupils was over 2 per cent (West, 1994b, p.13). However, Stephens thinks that not too much should be read into this growth rate: he notes that

> 'despite what has been said of the growth of working-class demand, all the evidence suggests that *only some form of compulsion* combined with state assistance could bring what was generally considered as adequate schooling [to the poorest children]' (Stephens, 1987, p.52 – emphasis added).

41

If compulsion is required, then this must be because of negative parental or child attitudes towards schooling. In fact, when Stephens's evidence is surveyed, it is not clear how he is able to arrive at this conclusion regarding the necessity of compulsion. *First*, he is able to offer many reasons for positive parental attitudes to schooling. He notes that not only were there economic benefits to schooling, but there were also political and social ones. There was the desire to be respectable in the eyes of 'local clergy and others' (p.49), as well as the attractions of 'reading for pleasure and the ability to communicate with relations living at a distance'. Moreover,

> 'as schooling became the norm the completely unschooled became increasingly untypical, a situation which must have brought its own pressure to conform... From 1840 schooling appears increasingly desirable socially and also functionally advantageous in an increasing number of jobs.' (pp.50-51)
>
> 'Moreover, the vast expansion from the 1830s of didactic evangelical and utilitarian publications, of political and commercial literature, and of newspapers, radical and otherwise, attest to a working-class society in which the ability to read must have added to the economic advantages political and social ones.' (p.51)

This trend in schooling norms would have a considerable bearing on the thesis that compulsion would be necessary to ensure an adequate education for all. If there were social and political, as well as economic, advantages in sending children to school, and if there were norms that made this more favourable, then it is likely the rate of schooling would continue to increase. However, let us ignore this (substantial) part of Stephens's evidence – which would provide strong support to West's argument – and continue to attempt to undermine West's argument.

Negative Attitudes to Schooling? Four Reasons

What are the negative attitudes of parents that Stephens says would need state compulsion to overcome? And what were the reasons for these attitudes? Reviewing his evidence, there seem to be *four* main reasons given. *Three* of these concern economic factors which may have influenced parental choice about sending children to school. The *first* is the fees for schooling, while the *second* is the *opportunity costs* of sending children to school, that is, the benefits forgone of children's income and assistance around the house that could be had if children had not gone to school. Both of these are likely to have been a considerable deterrent to many poor parents. Stephens notes: 'Certainly not all families were able to view the loss of children's earnings with equanimity' (p.52). Moreover, he notes the remarks of Revd. J.P. Norris (HMI, 1850s), who suggests that school fees were far less important than the opportunity costs: parents 'cannot afford *to give up the value of their child's time*... the school fee is a mere trifle' (quoted on p.128). These first two factors would be influenced by poverty; and Stephens points out that 'Poverty was, indeed, the main reason given' by working-class parents for not sending children to school (p.25).

Third, another economic factor would relate to the economic benefits that were considered to be obtained from schooling. It may well be that many parents could see no economic benefit to be derived from schooling for their children, and so were not prepared to make the necessary sacrifices for no economic return. Stephens notes that for some parents, their relative prosperity did not depend on schooling, and they did not see why it would for their children either. It was important for some children to learn manual dexterity early on, and

'in the iron and coal districts there were many prosperous employers who had risen from the lowest occupations in the pit, the furnace or the forge, and even the nailers' shop without ever acquiring the rudiments of reading or writing' (p.123).

A common saying, he notes, was: 'The father went down the pit and he made a fortune, his son went to school and lost it' (p.123). This attitude was reinforced by some employers:

'[E]ven employers active in promoting schooling admitted that their most skilful and best paid workmen were not necessarily those who were literate' (p.124).

Moreover, when parents preferred to send their children to vocational schools, again this could have been for sound economic factors:

'The lace and plait schools, so disliked by contemporary educationalists and philanthropists, could be regarded less as evidence of parental exploitation than indicative of parental responsibility in securing for their children the practical

43

education of the apprentice in crafts where skills had necessarily to be mastered at an early age' (p.175).

Each of these three reasons depends upon economic factors. Our interest is in whether or not these factors would have continued to be of importance towards the end of the 19th and in the 20th century. Clearly, if the wealth of the nation had continued to increase, the importance of the first two of these factors is likely to have rapidly diminished. The third factor is clearly influenced by the demands of employment, and Stephens observes that as industrialisation increased, the demands of employers for a schooled, skilled workforce likewise increased. A survey in the 1840s found that employers in Nottinghamshire, Derbyshire, Leicestershire and Birmingham unanimously agreed that education led to workers who were

'more trustworthy, more respectful ... more accessible to reason in disputes over wages or changes in routine, better conducted in their social duties, and more refined in their tastes and use of language' (p.136, quoting Parliamentary Papers of 1843).

Again, there seemed to be very strong pressures from industry for educated workers, pressures that would have found their way down to parents and children. Similar views were expressed in other parts of the country and at later times. There were also technical advantages of a better educated workforce, in metal, pottery and textile trades, although not in the coal and iron industries (p.137). An uneducated workforce led to 'the loss of immense sums of money' (p.137).

Indeed, all this evidence can be put into a broader context. Osterfield notes a commonly-observed phenomenon of modernisation: 'In a pre-industrial society children support their parents; in an industrial society parents support their children' (Osterfield, 1992, p.117). Children cease to be the 'economic assets they were in pre-industrial society', instead becoming economic liabilities. In pre-industrial societies, 'the cost of rearing children is minimal and by the time they are 5 or 6 years old they are working in the fields or doing other odd jobs and more than "paying their way"' (p.113). More children means an increased supply of food, and the only support for parents in old age. However, in a modern industrialised society, skills for work often require years of formal training, and the incentives go the other way – wages are higher, it is possible to support families with only one or two wages, and it is necessary for children to be dependent for longer if they are to have the skills required to obtain highly-paid employment. So the flow of wealth goes from parents to children.

The *fourth* factor influencing parental attitudes towards education which Stephens notes *is* of a different, non-economic type. He observes that the middle-classes tended to overlook the three economic factors, instead criticising the working classes for parental greed and laziness. Some parents, it was reported, did live off their children's wages, but these were a small minority of reported cases (Stephens, 1987, p.126). There were also savage indictments of working-class drunkenness, with parents spending money on drink rather than on education of children. Now clearly, in these cases, it would seem that compulsion would have been necessary in order to ensure that these children received an adequate education. But to repeat: Stephens's evidence suggests they are likely to have been a very small minority of cases; moreover, given the discussion above about the process of modernisation, it is plausible that such attitudes would not have lasted very long as society became more industrialised.

What do these four factors and Stephens's evidence suggest about the need for compulsion after 1870? The first three factors were the most significant, but it is highly likely that all four would have become less significant as the society grew in wealth and modernisation. However, even if there were some parents who would not themselves be interested in sending children to school, they are likely to have remained in a small minority. At most, Stephens's evidence warrants the conclusion that very selective compulsion of a few parents would have been necessary as the wealth of the people grew, not wholesale universal compulsion as he suggests.

Without the State

This brief survey of evidence surrounding the situation in England and Wales in the 19th century suggests that without the state, very great educational opportunities were provided. A very substantial piece of evidence in support of this, not already considered, is that Forster introduced his 1870 Bill *explicitly* as a measure to cater for those children not covered by existing voluntary measures. It was *not* designed to cater universally for all children. Moreover, under the Act, the country was divided into school districts, a survey of the educational needs of each district conducted, and non-state sources given six months to rectify the deficiencies (Reid, [1888], 1970, pp.479, 506). Clearly, Forster was aware that voluntary private provision was a very valuable resource in educational provision, and needed to be supplemented as required, not replaced.

Moreover, England and Wales were not unique in this respect. There is similar evidence from America (High and Ellig, 1992), and from Scotland. The Scottish example is usually held up to show the opposite. For example, Kiesling castigates West's discussion of the importance of private finance in 19th-century schooling in Scotland:

> 'The Scottish educational system, with well-paid schoolmasters in parish schools funded by taxes on large landowners was quite different from the situation in England and Wales' (Kiesling, 1983, p.425).

However, as West points out, by the end of the 19th century the Scottish system had been rendered insufficient by the growth of population. In 1818, private unendowed schools were taking two-thirds of all pupils, the parish schools only a third (see West, 1983, p.429, and West, 1970, p.74). And these figures excluded Sunday schools, Dame schools and schools for the rich. Very little of this education was free, whether in the private or parish schools.

This is all evidence from the 19th century. However, strong supporting contemporary evidence for the possibilities of education without the state can also be found. Where state education is perceived to be inadequate, in countries across the globe people respond by 'plugging the gaps'. In deprived inner-city areas in the UK, for example, private groups have moved to set up 'Saturday Schools', operating in church halls or community centres, where children who are not benefiting from day schooling learn basic mathematics and English. Sometimes private schools have opened in these areas, specifically to cater for these deprived and disadvantaged people who are not satisfied by the state system, operating on a shoe-string budget, and asking small fees. A huge number of projects sponsored by business to supplement or replace unsatisfactory state schooling has also emerged in response to weaknesses in the system. These include Community Service Volunteers' (CSV) Changemakers project, sponsored by, *inter alia*, Business in the Community, which aims to tackle the problems of youth 'truancy, delinquency and crime', aiming to enable young people to 'acquire the habits of good citizenship' and develop employability skills (Mulligan, 1994). Other similar projects in the UK include Barclay's New Futures, Inter-Action, BP Student Tutoring, Young Enterprise, Education Extra, and the Youth Award Scheme.

In the USA, the National Foundation for Teaching Entrepreneurship (NFTE) was set up on the initiative of one entrepreneur, now sponsored by a wide range of business and philanthropic interests, specifically to educate 'at risk' young people who were dropping out of the state school system in New York; its influence has spread across America, to the UK (where Businesswise now follows its lead), to Eastern Europe, and to South Africa. The Edison Project was established as a direct response to the perceived failures of state schooling, to create a nation-wide system of private schools available to all, which emphasise high standards and discipline, and incorporate technological advances.

Finally, in apartheid South Africa, because of the extremely poor quality of government-provided schooling for blacks, and widespread political disruption of schools, educational entrepreneurs and philanthropists responded to parental and student frustration, providing alternative educational services. Perhaps the most extreme example was of the booming business in Johannesburg, where over 2,000 children were accommodated in a disused warehouse. Older children were taught in small groups, relaying this to larger groups of younger children – just like the Lancastrian schools in Victorian England. Other examples abounded: the First National College of South Africa, in a disused office block between Soweto and Johannesburg, had strict discipline, and expected the highest standards; in the rural areas there were numerous 'shack' schools, run along similar lines.

The crucial thing to remember about all these examples is that, although state schooling is free in all the countries mentioned, either poor parents prefer to skimp and save to give their children alternative, more satisfactory, educational opportunities, or business and philanthropy recognises the need to fund alternatives to the state system. Just as in

Victorian England and Wales, families, philanthropy and business see that it is worth making sacrifices in order to ensure children have access to high quality educational opportunities. In many cases, these opportunities are pursued in spite of, not because of, state intervention.

Without the state, private interests are able to provide substantial schooling. The 'Far Side' cartoon mentioned at the beginning of this chapter would not reflect the realities of education without the state, of a real market in education. Which brings us back to the thought experiment of the previous chapter. Is it not reasonable to suppose that, just as in the genuine example of educational markets in England and Wales, the great majority of families in the market model *would* be 'educationally concerned' and able to fund educational opportunities? Given the growth in *per capita* income since the 19th century, it could be expected that the proportion of families would be at least as high as that found by West, and without the geographical inconsistencies suggested by Stephens. Even if the exact figure was disputed, the notion that the majority of families would be concerned about their children's education, and would find funds to provide for it, and that suppliers would adapt educational opportunities suitably, is supported by the historical evidence from England and Wales. For the minority not thus provided for, there could, at the most, be a minimal rôle for the state in funding and selective compulsion.

We have had two attempts at finding a justification for the state to override markets in education. Both pointed to some rôle, in terms of funding and compulsion for a minority. The issue of the curriculum and the information problem have not yet been addressed, so these may bring some additional rôle for government. But there will be many other objections to the market model portrayed. We now turn to the most important of these.

4 | Equality, Equity and Educational Markets

Whatever the merits of the market model of the thought experiment, as it stands it may fail to convince many of those who are against markets in education. The historical evidence notwithstanding, their objections to markets are still waiting to be answered; indeed, they are presumably brought into stark relief by our thought experiment.

As mentioned earlier, there is a vast international literature critical of moves towards 'markets' in education. The foremost objections in the educational literature are that markets would not provide equality of opportunity or promote equity; that markets break the links between education and democracy, including the need for democratic control of the curriculum; and that parents and children are ill-equipped to choose in the educational market.

In this chapter, I tackle the issues of equality and equity; in the next, the curriculum. Discussion of the latter will bring in the information argument and raise some of the important issues concerning democracy (for extended arguments on these and related arguments, see Tooley, 1994, 1995a, 1995b, 1996).

Educationists' Critique of Markets

Recent arguments show the issue of equality to be of particular concern to educationists in their objections to markets. For example, Ball attacks markets because:

> 'inequality is not only inevitable but *necessary* in the market in order to provide differential rewards which will stimulate competition and produce incentives' (Ball, 1990a, pp.2-3).

Levitas bemoans that market provision

> 'would, *of course*, lead to far greater inequalities of opportunities within the education system' (Levitas, 1986, p.84 – emphasis added).

49

Ranson stresses that

'Under the guise of neutrality, the institution of the market actively confirms and reinforces the pre-existing social order of wealth and privilege' (Ranson, 1990, p.15).

Jonathan argues that if educational provision is left to the market, there will be

'a further twist to the spiral of cumulative advantage and disadvantage which results when the state is rolled back to enable "free and fair" competition between individuals or groups who have quite different starting points in the social race' (Jonathan, 1989, p.323).

There would seem to be two ways of approaching these objections. One way would be to point to the possible trade-offs between equality and other important factors. In the economic literature the trade-off is normally considered to be between equality and efficiency (for example, Barr, 1993, Ch.4); in philosophical literature the trade-off is between equality and liberty (for example, De Jasay, 1990). Detailed arguments could then be made outlining why the trade off might come down on the side of markets, for reasons of efficiency or liberty, even if this would lead to a less equitable distribution. This could be argued on the grounds of classical liberalism, focusing on the primary importance of personal liberty, and the undesirability of expanding the powers of the state.

However, to pursue the argument in this way would be both to concede too much, and also to run the risk of not winning any converts, not least amongst the opponents of markets in education mentioned above. We would be conceding too much, because it may be the assumption cannot be made so easily that state intervention can provide equality whereas markets cannot. As for converts, it seems likely that those objecting to markets have already decided that equality or equity should carry greater weight than liberty or efficiency, and so outlining the opposite perspective might not be fruitful.

My method, instead, will be to attempt to treat the objections sympathetically from the basis on which they have been put forward. Is it possible that, *even for those who hold equality to be of primary importance*, the market model is much more satisfactory than *prima facie* it appears, and more satisfactory at achieving equality than the state?

An Empirical Argument

The first step in this argument is empirical. Many of those objecting to markets on these grounds seem to forget that there were widespread concerns about inequality over the last 30 or 40 years, well before there were any purported market reforms on the agenda. In the USA, for example, the seminal studies showing widespread inequality within the state schooling system were Coleman *et al.*(1966) and Jencks *et al.* (1971). In the UK, similar inequalities were found by Rutter *et al.* (1979). More recently, Marks and Pomian-Srzednicki (1985, p.11) found that students in comprehensive schools in one local education authority (LEA) could, on average, obtain more than twice as many exam passes as their counterparts of similar social class in another LEA; Smith and Tomlinson (1989) showed that

> 'different secondary schools achieve substantially different results with children who are comparable in terms of background and attainment at an earlier time. They also show that these school effects are far more important than any differences in attainment between black and white children' (p.3).

Chubb and Moe (1990) showed similar huge unequal school effects in the USA; Barr (1993, pp.361-65) usefully summarises the inequity of state education in the UK.

Schooling has never been equal, even within neighbourhoods. It is not a secret that property prices have reflected school catchment areas, with wealthier parents able to buy into better school districts and hence reinforce social inequality.

But this is not a complete rebuttal of the empirical case: for in the literature there is an additional argument not just that markets would lead to inequality, but that in various countries – New Zealand, Australia and the UK in particular – inequality *has* increased because of recent reforms. Moreover, the aspects of the current reforms that are blamed are those purportedly concerned with markets. Now, I am not sure that the evidence does show an increase in inequality at all (see, for example, my review of Walford, 1994, in Tooley, 1995c). But even if it did, would it show that markets – the kinds of markets in education which we have been discussing in our thought experiment – are to be damned? It would not. Not only have the reforms not brought in markets in the sense we are considering, but, *from a market perspective*, it would not be surprising if inequality *had* increased with the reforms that have been introduced. Crucially, this would be because government is still very much in control, not because control has been ceded to markets. In terms of the schema introduced in Chapter 1, government has not relinquished control over (direct) funding or provision, and, while some regulation has been relaxed, other, heftier regulation has been imposed.

A Three-School Neighbourhood Example

Consider a neighbourhood, say, with three schools, and with educational reform similar to that of the 'school choice' reforms introduced around the world. That is, some reform of the demand side has taken place, with money following students, and open enrolment, allowing parental choice of school; the supply side is still very restricted, however, it being very difficult to open an educational institution, and with all state schools subject to stiff regulations, perhaps including a national curriculum, national testing, league tables, inspection and teacher certification. No price mechanisms have been introduced. Critics claim that the schools are in competition, but this is not true in the market sense. For the competitive pressures are not great: if a school is not doing well, it will not very likely be closed or have any market pressure brought to bear. If it does *very* badly, then it might have a government task force come to help it out, perhaps bringing more resources. Moreover, teachers in a failing school receive exactly the salaries of staff in a successful school.

Suppose that one of these three schools becomes much better than the others, or is perceived to be so. It becomes over-subscribed. Suppose too that the others become less popular, and worse, as the critics maintain would happen. The more popular school is not allowed to expand (perhaps because of the rules regarding 'surplus places'), nor is it allowed to select pupils by academic attainment. It turns to interviewing parents, or operating a strict geographical selection criterion, or giving preference to the siblings of existing pupils.

All of these, of course, increase the unfairness of the procedure, because if you do not live in the neighbourhood (perhaps because property prices have been pushed up) or do not have articulate parents, then it is unlikely you will be admitted to the popular school. But those who have enough money, or are more concerned, are likely to send their children away from the neighbourhood schools altogether. So two of the schools in the neighbourhood are likely to be deprived of better motivated youngsters, and may well go into decline. There is a lot of sense in critics' arguments along these lines. But the crucial point is: Is this the market operating? Or would a more authentic market be better?

Results of an Authentic Market

Such a market would have completely different results. The demand-side mechanisms would bring real market pressure to bear to force up standards – exactly as real market pressure ensures the three supermarkets in my neighbourhood keep up high standards of quality. So, with genuine market mechanisms, 'there is a real incentive for schools to vie with one another both in the excellence of their "product" and in the reduction of its cost' (Peacock and Wiseman, 1964, p.46), and the problem of the deteriorating schools might not arise at all.

Moreover, the market liberation of the supply side would make an important difference too, avoiding the inequity of the current system. If the worst-case scenario happened, and the demand-side pressures were not enough to keep some of the schools from failing, then the most popular school could do what any other successful business can do. That is not to turn custom away, but to expand, perhaps by taking over a failing school, and bringing in successful ethos and practices, or by opening new outlets. Even if the successful business did not want to expand, other educational entrepreneurs could see the market niche brought about by a failing school with dissatisfied customers, and establish new, more appropriate educational settings for those people.

Furthermore, with a liberated supply side, one sort of school would not necessarily attract as many young people as the most popular school does at present, because a wide variety of educational settings would be available and seen as increasingly attractive. The currently popular academic school might attract all those students who are good at languages, arts, sciences, practical subjects, and those whose parents simply want them to be rubbing shoulders with those who are good at these things. But with the supply side opened up, there would develop specialist educational settings: perhaps a language school, a science academy, somewhere with a reputation for helping slow learners, and so on. All of these would cater for different markets, and would undermine the possibility of one institution being so much more popular than the others.

The point is that it is not surprising if there is inequality in current 'choice' systems. This has nothing to do with 'markets', but everything to do with rigid state intervention which discourages innovation and enterprise.

Given this suggestion, it might seem we are at an impasse with the empirical step in the argument. We do have evidence of inequality in state education, and evidence and a logical argument (above) to show how inequality, perhaps even increasing inequality, could be the result of recent educational reforms. But this is not evidence about markets, because the relevant reforms do not bring in aspects of genuine markets. Indeed, we have no evidence about the impact of markets on educational equality, because nowhere is there a market in education[1] operating.

Why Equality?

Given this empirical impasse, a second argument could be fruitful. Thus far we have been assuming that, once weights have been attached to the aims of policy in terms of equality, efficiency or liberty, it is a technical, empirical matter to decide the best methods for achieving those aims; that is, 'Whether a given aim should be pursued by market allocation or by public provision depends on which of these methods more nearly achieves in some instances' (Barr, 1993, p.4). However, this approach misses out an important preliminary question. Instead of taking the desire for equality at face value, it is important to ask *why* this aim is being sought,

---

[1] This must not be taken to mean that my position is, in the Popperian sense, unfalsifiable: we could stipulate what markets in education would look like, and agree on some measures of equality. If more authentic markets in education were brought in, we could then discover what impact they have on equality.

what it is that is desirable about equality which makes it a desideratum of educationists. It is far too easy to latch on to the term 'equality', or 'equity', and it is not always clear that everyone knows exactly what is being sought and why.

To focus the discussion, we turn to the work of economists and philosophers whose arguments have been used, and are likely to continue to be used, to buttress the case against markets on grounds of equality or equity. In fact, when the arguments are examined, they do not seem to support the case against markets after all. Indeed, they can plausibly be used to support a case against universal state intervention.

This is counter-intuitive; let us be clear why. If equality is the aim, then it is obvious, the argument would go, that markets cannot deliver it. For equality is intuitively understood in a literal sense as meaning roughly 'without difference', and there are clear differences between people's wealth and circumstances, which will be reflected in their market choices. Similarly, the converse also seems intuitively as obvious. The state, and only the state, has the coercive powers which could be used to redistribute wealth, so that differences between people's circumstances are *not* reflected in their market choices. It might entail more coercion than we have ever seen thus far, might offend liberty or efficiency more than is felt to be tolerable by many, but that is not the point: it seems intuitively *possible* for state intervention to work towards this end in a way not conceivable for the market. What is possible in our market model, as we saw in Chapter 2, is for there to be state intervention for the poor, a 'priority principle', where attention is given only to those who are needy, but not to others.

Interestingly, however, when we turn to the writings of these economists and philosophers as to why equality is desired, the impression clearly comes through that it is actually something rather close to the 'priority principle' that is sought, not equality in any literal sense. This has very important implications for the ethics of markets in education, as we shall see.

Economists on Equality

For example, the economists Nicholas Barr and Julian Le Grand both agree that the concept of equality or equity is 'elusive' (Barr, 1993, p.147), unlike the concept of efficiency, which can be defined easily in economic terms. However, after exploring difficulties with defining equality in terms of equal final income, equality of public expenditure on different individuals, equality in the use or cost of welfare, and equality of outcome, Barr then settles for a definition of equality of opportunity,[2] while Le Grand focuses on a definition of equity.[3] As far as educational implications are concerned, Barr argues that equality of opportunity implies that

> 'if individuals A and B have similar tastes and ability, they should receive the *same* education, irrespective of factors which are thought to be irrelevant, e.g. income' (Barr, 1993, p.337 – emphasis added).

Similarly, Le Grand argues that what is inequitable in terms of education is where 'children from poor families receive *less* education than those from rich ones' (Le Grand, 1991, p.86), suggesting again that it is the *same* education which is required.

However, nowhere do they argue explicitly why it is the 'same', that is, an 'equal' education that is desired, nor indeed what is meant by that term. Have they intended these words to be used in the literal sense we noted earlier, or would they be happy with something analogous to the 'priority' usage?

---

[2] For Barr, equality of opportunity pertains 'if the expected value of money income is the same for all individuals with given T [taste] characteristics, but must be invariant to their D [discrimination – social class, race, sex, parental money income] characteristics' (Barr, 1993, p.147).

Even here, he admits that there are severe problems with his definition in terms of how full income is measured, and the crucial difference between Taste and Discrimination characteristics. The particular problem is 'natural ability': should this come under T or D? If it is innate, then society might baulk at confiscating wealth accrued from the development of particular talents; if it is not, then education and upbringing would have an input, and hence it could be conceived as a D characteristic.

[3] Le Grand (1991) argues that the essential feature of inequity is when 'individuals receive less than others because of factors *beyond their control*' (p.86). So equity is satisfied if 'informed individuals' are able to choose over '*equal* choice sets' (p.87 – emphasis added), where a 'choice set' is a set of possibilities bounded by 'constraints', and 'constraints' are factors beyond individual control. The 'informed' part of the definition will be addressed later.

What do they mean by the 'same' or 'equal' education? This raises a difficult measurement problem. We would need to know two individuals' 'full education' before we could ascertain whether their education was 'equal'. But, just as there are great difficulties with the measurement of 'full income', in part because 'non-money income' is largely unmeasurable (Barr, 1993, p.135), so too there is a problem with measuring 'full education', in part because 'non-school education' is so difficult to measure. Focusing on schooling only has at least the virtue of a possible solution, even if it cuts out a huge swathe of the educational process. But even considering schooling alone raises other problems. What aspects of schooling are required to be 'equal'?

Clearly, our two economists cannot have in mind that there should be equal schooling *outcomes*, because they recognise that young people have different levels of motivation (Barr, 1993, p.337; Le Grand, 1991, p.86), and this, interacting with abilities, will be reflected in different outcomes. Perhaps they have in mind equal educational (schooling) resources?[4] But, it should be recalled, the school effectiveness literature mentioned above (for example, Smith and Tomlinson, 1989, Chubb and Moe, 1990) shows that the 'same' resources can lead to vastly different educational outcomes. It is the way resources *are used* which is important, not the resources themselves.

Moreover, the discussion in our thought experiment in Chapter 2 also has a bearing here. For example, suppose the two young people *A* and *B* have similar 'tastes and ability' but *B* (who comes from the richer background) is taught in a school which has many more resources than *A*'s school. It might seem that this contrast is objectionable on the grounds of equality or equity. But suppose that the wealthier school uses its resources on expensive older graduate teachers and luxurious surroundings, while *A* is educated less expensively using fewer teachers, networked multimedia systems and community service, as in the thought experiment. Would this be objected to on grounds of equality or equity by Barr or Le Grand? Presumably, they would want to know more about the education of *A* and *B* before they could pass any judgement. For the fact of unequal resources alone would tell us nothing

---

[4] Le Grand is influenced by Dworkin, and equality of resources is what he seeks. Dworkin's argument is addressed shortly.

about the educational opportunities being offered to the young people.

Perhaps 'the same' education means the same *curriculum*, understood broadly to include the ethos and organisation of educational settings? Again, there would be great difficulties, akin to the measurement of full income, which would inhibit the measuring of whether individuals had been offered the same curriculum, even if a compulsory curriculum was imposed by government. (This would include such difficulties as individuals' different attention spans, reaction to specific teachers, teachers understanding of the curriculum requirements, and so on). In any case, the next chapter will argue against the possibility of government intervention in the curriculum – suggesting that it is not desirable that government should intervene to ensure sameness in this way, these other difficulties notwithstanding.

Perhaps what Barr and Le Grand, and others, have in mind is that 'the same' education is needed simply to avoid the following rather obvious inequity: As things stand, young people whose parents can afford to send their children to the better private schools will have social advantages, including great opportunities for networking, a sure route to a top university, and thence an advantage over less fortunate people in applying for the limited number of 'top jobs'. If this was felt to be an objection (and it is the 'positionality' objection to educational markets of Miliband, 1991, and Jonathan, 1990), then it falls into at least two traps.

First, it vastly over-estimates the potential of schooling in any social engineering project. For suppose that state intervention could somehow make the schooling opportunities of rich and poor families equal, would this rule out the influence of the family in the pursuit of the 'limited goods' such as 'top jobs'? Of course not: indeed, the paradox would be that, the more equal schooling becomes, the more important would family connections and influence become in the competition for limited goods. If middle-class families cannot buy into better schools, we can be sure that they would buy into opportunities outside schools, and use the full weight of their influence to secure networking contacts which will help in the competition for the limited goods.[5]

---

[5] I have explored this paradox of positionality in more detail elsewhere (see Tooley, 1995a, pp.18-21).

Second, to think thus would be to ignore the lessons of the information revolution, and the implications of ideas put forward in the thought experiment. For access to greater opportunities for networking does *not* necessarily mean much expense. It may not have been true even historically – for many good grammar schools in England and Wales were able to send young people to Oxford and Cambridge, while spending much less than private schools. But information and networking is now cheap. Perhaps the young person at a less expensive school or educational setting will be networking through the internet with top professors and influential people around the world – as an ordinary part of his or her education. It is possible for young people to do this now; under more authentic educational markets it would very likely be an obvious educational tool.

Given these factors, rather than looking for 'equal' or the 'same' education, Barr and Le Grand, and others, should rather be seeking to judge whether there are *adequate educational opportunities* for all individuals to develop their talents. The 'same' or 'equal' notion is a distraction in their arguments.

Philosophers on Equality

Perhaps we have expected too much of economists in their conceptual analysis; presumably when we turn to the arguments of *philosophers*, we will discover what it is about 'equality' that is desirable, and why markets in education could not possibly satisfy this. On the contrary, however, it seems that the arguments of influential philosophers continue to offer support for our position.

For example, perhaps the most celebrated moral and social philosopher this century, John Rawls, created his elaborate system of the original position and the 'veil of ignorance', *not* as it turns out, to ensure literal equality. Indeed, he is quite clear that this will not arise, but that, under his 'principles of justice', some inequalities are permissible, providing that they are 'arranged so that they are ...to the greatest benefit of the least advantaged' (Rawls, 1972, p.302). Crucially, Rawls explicitly argues that his principles are important in order to *guarantee a 'satisfactory minimum' standard of living for all* (p.156). Whether or not they achieve this is another matter; the crucial point is that this is his aim, to ensure that a level of 'adequacy' is attained for all, not that there should be equality.

Ronald Dworkin's influential argument, building on Rawls', arrives at a similar position. We do not need to look to his complex four-part work (1981a, 1981b, 1987, 1988) setting out his theory of 'equality of resources' to ascertain why equality is sought, because there he is only interested in *defining* a suitable conception of equality of resources, and not in defending it' (1981b, p.283). Oddly, however, even when he explicitly entitles a paper 'Why Liberals Should Care about Equality' (1985), nowhere does he actually explain why liberals, or anyone else, should indeed care. However, although there are no explicit comments, there are hints as to what the problem with inequality is. Again, these reveal that it is *not* inequality as such that Dworkin is actually worried about, but, again, a notion of adequacy. For example, he worries that in the United States:

'A substantial minority of Americans are chronically unemployed or earn wages below any realistic "poverty line" or are handicapped in various ways or burdened with special needs' (Dworkin, 1985, p.208).

Moreover:

'The children of the poor must not be stinted of education or otherwise locked into positions at the bottom of society' (p.211).

But note that here his problem is not that this minority earns *less* than others, that there is inequality, but that they live in poverty, that they do not have enough. So he has illegitimately jumped from showing that it is important that everyone has the 'means to lead a life with choice and value' (p.212) to arguing that everyone should have equality of resources. This is clearly too big a jump, one not afforded by his arguments.[6]

Similarly, White (1994) explores the arguments of other political philosophers, Nagel, Nielsen and Norman,[7] and comes up with a similar conclusion:

---

[6] Further details on the inadequacy of Dworkin's and Rawls's arguments can be found in Tooley, 1995a, Ch.2.

[7] The alliteration was, I am sure, purely coincidental!

'Why is a society where all are equal, or much less unequal ... desirable in itself?... I have yet to see an adequate answer to this question. Even recent defences of egalitarianism in the philosophical literature do not provide one' (White, 1994, p.173).

Moreover, White notes that several philosophers are now explicitly claiming that it is something like 'adequacy' which is the only viable interpretation of equality. Frankfurt (1988), for example, argues:

'To show of poverty that it is compellingly undesirable does nothing whatsoever to show the same of inequality. For what makes someone poor in the morally relevant sense – in which poverty is understood as a condition from which we naturally recoil – is not that his economic assets are simply of lesser magnitude than those of others' (Frankfurt, 1988, p.147).

Similarly, Raz (1986) has come to the position that it is not inequality as such which is undesirable, but inadequacy:

'[W]hat makes us care about various inequalities is not the inequality but the concern identified by the underlying principle. It is the hunger of the hungry, the need of the needy, the suffering of the ill, and so on. ... our concern for the hungry, the needy, the suffering, and not our concern for equality, makes us give them the priority' (Raz, 1986, p.240).

Thus there is a respectable tradition in moral philosophy which points to an interpretation of equality, or equity, as meaning 'adequate opportunities for all'. Moreover, even when this is not the intention, supposedly egalitarian philosophers can be seen as, in reality, arguing for it.

There is one final aspect of the argument concerning equality which might be seen as a crucial objection to markets. Rather than the problems we have encountered above, or in addition to them, it might be argued that markets in education would not satisfy the demand for 'political equality'. This issue is addressed in the next chapter, which considers democratic control of the curriculum.

Markets in Education and the Promotion of Equality

Markets in education have been roundly condemned in the educational literature because they would undermine equality or equity. This paper has argued that state intervention in education has never yet been able to achieve equality. It has also argued that the supposed empirical evidence gathered to show markets increase inequality is only evidence of state intervention increasing equality. The so-called markets have hardly moved at all from a position of detailed state regulation, direct funding and provision; their obvious disadvantages are the result of the continuing state influence, not the result of any mild market incentives that have been introduced.

Given the lack of evidence, we tried a different tack, exploring what is desirable about equality or equity. Using arguments of philosophers and economists, we have shown that a permissible interpretation of equality or equity is as 'adequacy'. Not only are some philosophers arguing for this explicitly, but it seems to underlie what other philosophers and economists find desirable, even if they do not argue the position themselves.

With this interpretation to hand, when we come to assess the ethics of markets in education, we find the goal-posts have moved. The previous question was: Can markets ensure equality in education? This question has now been transformed to: Can markets ensure adequate educational opportunities for all? This can usefully be spelled out as three sub-questions:

- Can markets ensure educational opportunities?

- Can markets ensure educational opportunities *for all*?

- Can markets ensure *adequate* educational opportunities for all?

It might also be thought that we need to address the parallel question: 'Can state intervention ensure adequate educational opportunities for all?', and that if the answer was in the affirmative, this would undermine the case being made here. However, the asymmetry is deliberate. One of the strongest objections to markets in education concerns equality. But if markets can ensure this without state intervention, then the argument for state intervention is undermined, *whether or not states could also ensure equality*. For, *ceteris paribus*, there would be other reasons to prefer markets, explained already, including economic reasons such as improved efficiency, innovation, incentives to improve quality, reduction of resources in the public sector, as well as ethical reasons such as their greater observance of liberty and autonomy. For the argument here, we are interested only in whether markets can ensure equality, irrespective of what governments can or cannot achieve.

Arguments against State Intervention: Empowering the Poor

However, that said, there do seem to be strong arguments undermining the possibility that democratic state intervention of the kind with which we are familiar (with state direct funding, provision and heavy regulation) *could* provide for adequate educational opportunities for all. One is found in the next chapter. A second powerful case is Goodin and Le Grand's critique of the welfare state:

> 'There was a time when many people in Britain believed that state provision of such services as health care, education, housing, even transport, free or at heavily subsidised prices, would in itself be a significant contribution to redistributing income to the poorest members of the community. ... These dreams were not fulfilled and it is important to understand the reasons. ... [There is] a large amount of evidence suggesting that most of the services mentioned actually benefit the middle classes at least as much as the poor, and in many cases more than the poor' (Goodin and Le Grand, 1987, p.91).

They give examples of the gross inequalities in state education, and suggest that these are an inevitable consequence of the middle-classes 'muscling in' on welfare, using the state to provide for their needs, at the expense of the poor. And, incidentally, while Goodin and Le Grand are pessimistic about any political ways of overcoming this, their economic solution entails introducing precisely the types of market mechanisms we have explored. The key, they argue, is for the poor to be given what we have called 'indirect funding' – vouchers or funds to be used for education – not for government to fund and provide universal education (p.223). Moreover, giving money (or vouchers) to the poor is likely to empower them:

> 'Primary distribution policies, by giving more economic resources to those who would otherwise be poor, give them more political resources, too. Secondary distribution policies, on the other hand,

often...benefit the non-poor and thus aid them in maintaining their economic and political hegemony' (p.235).

Finally,

> 'If the welfare state were *purely* a matter of helping those less well-off than themselves, then, paradoxically, the non-poor might support it even more strongly than if it were partly of benefit to themselves as well' (p.213).

So egalitarians, they say, should look at ways of correcting the primary income distribution, through indirect funding, rather than at enhancing universal state provision (p.236).

Adequate Educational Opportunities for All

We will return to these issues in .Chapter 5. Now, how do markets fare under the three sub-questions about ensuring educational opportunities for all? The arguments in the thought experiment (Chapter 2) and the historical excursion (Chapter 3) answer the first question in the affirmative. Historical evidence suggests markets will promote educational opportunities, and we see that, where state education is failing, entrepreneurs seize the opportunity to develop appropriate educational markets. There are no logical difficulties either which might undermine this response. As far as the second sub-question is concerned, the thought experiment and history suggested that markets could go a long way towards catering *for all*, but that there is likely to be a small residual which would not be so catered for. This would need, at most, some small amount of state intervention – deliberately constrained state intervention – which would ensure funds for those who were too poor, and selectively compel those who did not want to partake of educational opportunities. Although this is no longer the 'pure' market, as defined in Chapter 1, it has only moved very slightly away from that, with a small amount of government intervention in funding and regulation, but none in provision. This 'market-with-a-safety-net' *can* provide educational opportunities *for all*.

Finally, would the educational opportunities be *adequate*? There seem to be three areas of concern here. The *first* concerns the physical aspects of buildings, facilities, and so on. Because of the incentives to maintain and improve quality, as noted earlier, there should be no problem in markets providing an adequate education in these terms. Indeed, the suggestion is that, in this respect, it would be superior to state intervention in provision, because this would not be susceptible to the same incentives to raise quality.

Second, educationists would want to know that the *curriculum* is adequate. This would probably be their crucial concern in terms of adequacy, for they would object to something as important being decided on 'the vagaries' of markets. This is a particularly important issue, raised also by discussion in the thought experiment of Chapter 2, which will be addressed in the next chapter.

Third, ensuring the adequacy of educational opportunities raises the issue of the information needed by, and available to, consumers. Indeed, Barr argues that the case for public provision of education for reasons of equality (as well as efficiency) rests largely on the information problem:

> '[P]rivate consumption decisions [in education] are likely to be efficient and equitable only if families have sufficient information, and if they use it in the child's best interest. ... Some parents, maybe disproportionately in the higher socioeconomic groups, are capable of more informed decisions than the state; others make poorer decisions. If the quality of parental choice is systematically related to socioeconomic status and the effect is strong, then private allocation can be argued to be less equitable than state allocation, irrespective of the balance of argument about efficiency.' (p.349)

Interestingly, the solution to this problem again is for government intervention to regulate, *inter alia*, the curriculum and compulsory attendance (Barr, 1993, p.346). It does not necessarily require this intervention: for Barr, it is an empirical question whether 'parents *on average* make better or worse decisions than the state about their children's education?' (p.349), and whether this could be true of *all* parents, or only those of higher socio-economic status. However, in the next chapter we will explore the possibility that, far from being a purely empirical issue, this question gets to the heart of what we mean by education and hence the appropriate levels of decision-making regarding it.

Should the State Regulate the Curriculum?
We are not quite at an answer to the question of whether markets in education can satisfy equality (understood as

'adequacy'). There remains the crucial issue of whether governments need to insist on a compulsory curriculum, or on compulsory attendance, to ensure an adequate education for all. But notice an important repercussion of this. If it is felt that the only additional way government needs to intervene in the market model for the sake of equality is by means such as regulating the curriculum, then this would leave no justification for further government intervention, in provision or additional funding. The only possible state intervention justified thus far would be considerably less than anything known to present generations. Only a small amount of funding, and the possibility of some regulation – nothing more.

Other writers have arrived at a similar position. The renowned philosopher of education, John White, although not known for his affection towards markets, seems to have come to a similar stance. He writes:

> 'I can see no reason of principle why the State must own and run its own schools... The crucial thing, it seems to me, is not who owns a school, but whether the school conforms to certain criteria of adequacy – as regards health and safety, for instance, but also as regards aims and curricula' (White, 1994, p.122).

The next chapter examines this important issue of the justification of state regulation of the curriculum, and other areas.

5 | The Curriculum, Democracy, and Markets

Each of the arguments for markets has pointed to a need to examine the desirability of government intervention in the curriculum, and other regulatory matters to do with the quality of education. The issue was raised in the thought experiment of Chapter 2, and was raised again in the discussion of equality and equity in Chapter 4. So someone could have agreed with the discussion thus far, and still argue that there is a substantial rôle for government in enforcing a national curriculum, and possibly other regulation too. This chapter challenges the need for government regulation of the curriculum only. The arguments can be suitably adapted to argue against other government regulation to ensure educational quality, regarding teacher certification, and the requirements of compulsory schooling. (The arguments in the thought experiment, and the historical discussion can also be used against compulsory schooling.) However, to keep the discussion manageable, the focus in this chapter will be limited to the curriculum.

Lessons of the National Curriculum

In England and Wales there is considerable experience of the imposition of the National Curriculum. This experience will provide the framework for the discussion in this chapter of the desirability or otherwise of government intervention in the curriculum in general.

The National Curriculum was introduced by the 1988 Education Reform Act, under Margaret Thatcher's influence. In her memoirs, Lady Thatcher is clear that she only envisaged the most rudimentary of curriculum guidance:

'I wanted ... a basic syllabus for English, Mathematics and Science with simple tests to show what pupils knew. It always seemed to me that a small committee of good teachers ought to be able to pool their experience and write down a list of the topics and sources to be covered without too much difficulty. There

67

ought then to be plenty of scope left for the individual teacher to concentrate with children on the particular aspects of the subject in which he or she felt a special enthusiasm or interest' (Thatcher, 1993, p.593).

This seems almost touching in its naïveté, given the bureaucratic monstrosity that emerged. Five years later, the monster had to be tamed, with Sir Ron Dearing appointed to slim down the curriculum and simplify testing. But his proposals only led to an intensification of educationalists' frustration and anger. The English subject advisory committee protested strongly about the way its advice was ignored; the primary working group found itself 'profoundly dispirited' about the new curriculum for the under sevens (*The Times Educational Supplement*, 20 May 1994); the revised History curriculum was criticised, for not making significant events in British history compulsory (*The Times*, 28 February 1994), or for selling out to the 'Right' (*The Times Educational Supplement*, 4 March 1994); the original Mathematics working group publicly asked for the mathematical *status quo* to be maintained and the Dearing slim-down to be resisted; both the Centre for Policy Studies (a think tank originally set up by Thatcher) and the National Union of Teachers – peculiar bedfellows – condemned Dearing's proposals for still being over-bureaucratic and time-consuming. Now, with a relief, teachers have greeted the notion that there will be a moratorium on any additional changes to the National Curriculum for a further five years. This has led, however, to many educationalists jostling for curriculum influence when the moratorium time is up.

This experience reveals the two major problems which imposing a national curriculum – any national curriculum – brings: the problem of 'competing visions', and the 'knowledge' problem. To illustrate these, we can see how these problems would emerge given one of the suggestions for a revised national curriculum. Professor Michael Barber is one of those seeking to influence the direction of the future national curriculum (Barber, 1994). I am not suggesting that his is a particularly worked out model – I have chosen it partly because it is reminiscent of Thatcher's thumbnail sketch of what she saw as a desirable curriculum, and because he is a very influential figure in educational circles. How would the 'competing visions' and 'knowledge' problems emerge for him, should his curriculum ideas ever be translated into policy?

The Problem of 'Competing Visions'

Barber's national curriculum sketch specifies a small core of agreed knowledge including 'key events from British and world history, and a handful of great writers of the English language', as well as 'Core Skills and Experiences', that is, thinking skills, problem-solving, teamwork and innovation. The underlying aim of the curriculum is to 'create a humanity consistent with care for, and sustenance of, the planet' (Barber, 1994, p.351). Now, if everyone agreed on this common core curriculum, there would be no need to impose it on schools. So clearly, it must be that this common core is either likely to be controversial, or not what individuals or communities would themselves seek from schooling.[1]

Barber's notions are controversial. *First*, there is a big debate in the mainstream educational journals about the relevance of the skills mentioned (see, for example, Barrow, 1990 and 1987, Griffiths, 1987, and Smith, 1987). Moreover, the notion that there could be an agreed canon of great writers and important historical events suggests that Barber has not been paying attention to recent events. For the History and English curriculum committees have found extraordinary problems in trying to decide upon these canons to be imposed on schools. Particularly in a multi-cultural society, and where education is such a political football, these issues will be very controversial.

Finally, we can observe that when his environmental aim of 'sustenance of the planet' is translated into curriculum proposals, this also would be rather controversial. There are powerful and influential environmental lobbies, for example, which think that such sustenance entails drastic curbs on wealth-creating. Perhaps Barber would even go along with those, but then he risks alienating other big constituencies of potential support. Moreover, there are increasingly influential bodies who maintain that there is much environmental

---

[1] This assumes there are no co-ordination problems in bringing about desired outcomes. The usual arguments that there would be are based in game theory; I have argued elsewhere that these arguments do not undermine the likelihood of co-ordination occurring (Tooley, 1995a, Ch.6).

scaremongering and that 'sustenance of the planet' is better achieved through a system of property rights and market mechanisms (see, for example, Anderson and Leal, 1991, Bate and Morris, 1994, and Morris, 1995). Just as Thatcher's thumbnail sketch proved increasingly difficult to put into practice, so will Barber's.

Moreover, this is not the only curriculum suggestion being put forward as the five-year embargo on changing the current National Curriculum runs out. Indeed, there are some influential protagonists who claim that their particular form of government intervention in the curriculum is necessary in order for people to be able to make sense of their lives at all (O'Hear and White, 1991). This is not to mention those whose loyalty has been built up to the curricular *status quo*, or those who preferred the *status quo ante*, as well as those who argue for a more Nationalist national curriculum, or a more socialist one, and so on.

With all these disparate loyalties, the problem of competing visions looms large. For democracies around the world work by allocating decision-making rights to elected officials, where 'winners' have the right to make binding policies, and 'losers' are obliged to accept these policies, however much they oppose them. This of course has the corollary that political authority is *extremely valuable* because there are few checks on how, and over what, it can be exercised. Thus there is a strong incentive for interest groups to try to capture political authority.

This brings us to the fundamental problems of democratic control of education. Given the controversial nature of these curriculum proposals, there will be incentives for non-compliance. Hence, governments are likely to 'bureaucratise the implementation of policy', to reduce the discretion of teachers and parents (Chubb and Moe, 1990, p.40). Moreover, the problem of political uncertainty rears its ugly head: those who succeed in capturing power have it guaranteed only for a short time, so have incentives to insulate policies from future democratic control:

'The best way for groups to protect their achievements from the uncertainties of future politics, therefore, is through formalisation: the formal reduction or elimination of discretion, and the formal insulation of any remaining discretion from future political influence' (Chubb and Moe, 1990, pp.42-43).

70

Another pressure at work within democratic control is the need for compromises, that is:

'agreements among contending, often mutually suspicious, sides that can easily come apart over time if they are informal and subject to discretion' (p.44).

Opposing groups can insure against these dangers by formalising the agreement and making it legally enforceable. Chubb and Moe's examples include that of a nine-page federal government statute to provide aid to disadvantaged students generating 174 pages of statutory amendments (p.44). Closer to home, we have already noted the burgeoning of the National Curriculum and national testing of Thatcher's minimalist ideas.

Democracy and Imposition

Some might argue that this is pathologising the process of democratic control, and that, at the very least, the process can be applauded for giving 'the people' choice over the curriculum. One cannot hide behind such reassuring claims. As it works in this country at present, and elsewhere, it is painfully hard to pretend that the democratic process leads to people deciding on a particular aspect of education such as the curriculum. To remind ourselves of this, just consider how the current National Curriculum came onto the statute books in 1988. Since the 1970s there had been a debate about the benefits of a national curriculum. Ball (1990c) suggests the Department for Education and Science sought to bring about a national curriculum whichever party was in power – that is, *whichever way* people voted in the ensuing elections. As the 1987 election approached, party manifestos were drawn up. In the case of the 1987 elections, the details on the curriculum in the Conservative party manifesto, for example, covered half a paragraph. This hardly seems an adequate basis on which to inform a decision about such an important matter.

Next, each voter can vote only once and for one party. So each voter will have voted on a variety of issues in the General Election, and will have been forced to conflate his or her vote on the curriculum with that on other issues. Someone who approved one party's stand on the curriculum might still have voted against that party because he or she disapproved of other issues in the manifesto, and vice versa. So decisions about the curriculum are likely to inform the decisions of only a very small minority of voters, if indeed any. The process gets even further away from the democratic ideal, as the elected prime minister then selects a cabinet, and it is this cabinet that effectively sets the political agenda, with only a small amount of modification of that agenda by the Houses of Parliament.

Moreover, if we follow the passage of the National Curriculum legislation through the political process, we see how, increasingly, professional educationalists impinge upon the process at all levels: they influenced the formulation of legislation, via the civil service and lobbying of Parliament. It was these professional educational bodies which were entrusted with 'fleshing out' proposals, and carrying policies into schools. Ordinary people play no part in these deliberations. Moreover, the subsequent changes to the National Curriculum were not brought about by *popular* demand − at most they could be seen as succumbing to the demands of other rival interest groups to have their own particular image of the good life imposed upon schools. Which brings us back to Barber: what he would be seeking would be to *impose* his vision, and it would be disingenuous to soften this by suggesting that it will occur through the democratic process.

Now, I suspect that Barber would be amongst those who would agree that democracy as currently practised is flawed, and that this accusation of imposition is largely correct, if undesirable. (If he did not think this, and that imposing the curriculum was desirable, then the knowledge problem is the one to challenge his confidence in so doing.) But he would presumably be amongst those who would argue that, hand-in-hand with these educational reforms, it would be desirable to have reforms of democracy too, or that one could lead to the other. Eventually, perhaps he would argue − and others certainly do argue − that one could have a real democratic debate about the curriculum, and that the sorts of difficulties described above would disappear. I am personally far more circumspect about potential improvements to democracy, thinking that there are perhaps insurmountable problems arising from social choice and public choice theory (see Tooley, 1995a, Ch.5). But again, let us suppose that the optimist's approach is right, that improvements could be made which would overcome the imperfections of democracy noted above. Even under these rather optimistic assumptions, I would still argue that democratic control of curricula would not be as desirable as leaving them to markets.

Suppose it was possible to create a much more responsive participatory democracy, as favoured by many of those who are likely to criticise markets (see Ranson, 1993, for example). Suppose in this democracy, some educational reformers seek to impose their curricular vision on educational institutions. How would they set about this? Presumably, they would need to convince *the majority of people*, not the political parties, or people's representatives, but people themselves, of the worthiness of their ideas. Suppose they did obtain enough public support to secure a majority for their proposals. Unless there was a consensus, that would mean that some would object to these.

Now, there would seem to be two possibilities. Either those in disagreement will accept the policies as part of the democratic give-and-take – perhaps trying to change the policies through the democratic process. Or they might refuse to accept them and ignore the laws. In either case, even in this improved democracy, there are clear and severe problems with this process. In the first case, surely if the educational reformers value their policy prescriptions, and have expended tremendous effort and resources in getting a majority of people to accept them, will they not be tempted to insulate their policies from further democratic control, particularly as they know that if they do not, those who oppose them *are* likely to do so, should they get power over education policy? In the second case, there would be problems of non-compliance. The logic of both pressures is detailed bureaucratic prescription to be the unintended consequence, even in an improved democracy, exactly as in the sorts of democracies we are familiar with. Even in the improved democracy, Thatcher's curriculum nightmare would become Barber's, too.

Flexibility of the Market Alternative

Contrast this with the market alternative. Suppose it was not possible to have democratic control of education in our imaginary society – what could educational reformers like Barber do then? They could campaign in the market-place of ideas to convince as many people of the wisdom of their proposals as they could. Again, if they convinced everyone, everyone would willingly adopt the proposals they sought. If they convinced a majority of people, then a majority would adopt them, without the disadvantages of democratic control of the process. Notice that the minority does not need to be disconsolate now: they can carry on with whatever proposals they wanted, and do not need to try to wrestle back control later on. Moreover, even if they did not succeed in convincing a majority, then all would not be lost! For there would be nothing to stop a *minority* of educational settings following their proposals. In both these ways, proposals could be tried out, and if found successful, others might follow. Without democratic control, influencing education policy need not be a 'zero-sum game': all can be winners in the educational curriculum market.

It might be objected, moreover, that, of course, in the market-place, some higher-order values would not be attractive to people. Perhaps the great majority of people do not want to have a multicultural education, say, or education for environmental awareness, but this is only because they are selfish, and do not know what is best for their society's cohesiveness or sustainability. It is only through the coercive power of the state that these values can be promoted. But if this is admitted, then it would have to be accepted that in a more responsive democracy these higher-order values would also not be expressed. Markets are much more like responsive democracies in this respect at least – they demand that people are convinced of the value of the ideas on offer before they are taken up.

The suggestion here is that the 'competing visions' problem of democracy undermines the desirability of seeking to impose a national curriculum on educational settings; however, this does not rule out the desirability of educational reformers seeking to encourage these settings to take on their ideas, allowing them to be explored in the market-place of ideas.

Suppose that Barber or any other curriculum champion is not convinced by this argument, or is convinced that his or her particular vision is the right one to seek to impose. Perhaps equity demands it, because their ideas alone are needed to fulfil the demands of an 'adequate' range of choices. Or perhaps the demands of autonomy require it, because without all following their curriculum, people will not have the autonomous basis for living a life of choice and value. Then the 'knowledge' or, as it is often called in the economic and philosophical literature, 'epistemic' argument can challenge this position. The intuitive understanding behind this position is that it is rather arrogant of curriculum reformers to believe they have hit upon the right solution, to be legally imposed upon all children, given both the limitations on our knowledge, and the way knowledge about educational needs is dispersed in the community.

The Knowledge Argument

Suppose our curriculum reformers are tempted by the notion that their curriculum should be the one which gets applied to all schools. This is notwithstanding the problems of competing visions which will lead, it has been suggested, to an over-prescriptive bureaucratic burden on schools. Their curriculum is too important to be left to markets. The knowledge argument challenges them on this assumption.

The knowledge argument holds against any central planning, stressing the importance of markets as devices which enable people 'to act autonomously in their own personal knowledge – knowledge that is typically tacit and practical in form' (Gray, 1992, p.3). Without market pricing of assets, relative scarcities are unknowable. Hayek (1978) developed this argument to show that the importance of markets lies in their ability to economise on the scarce resource of human knowledge, dispersed through all of society. For Hayek,

> 'the most important rôle of the market is that of a device for the transmission and utilisation of unarticulated, and sometimes inarticulable, tacit and local knowledge' (p.8).

The market acts as a discovery process, 'developing and spreading otherwise unavailable, latent information' (De Jasay, 1990, p.11). While not necessarily being in sympathy with it, Pring acknowledges the persuasiveness of the argument:

> 'The tacit knowledge may be about local institutions or it may be about the kind of things they want and the values they have which they cannot convey to others explicitly. But it is manifested in the choices they make and in the values which they

recognise in the institutions they visit. The millions of decisions that people make based on such tacit knowledge must necessarily escape the planner.' (Pring, 1994, pp.38-39)

In order to relate this argument to government intervention in the curriculum, we need to focus on the nature of education. This illustrates why central planning of education is undesirable, and why it is the 'local' knowledge that people and teachers have which is crucial to the educational process. *First*, this is because education requires personal relationships and interactions, needing continual and immediate feedback. For education to take place, this requires simply that teachers, parents and students 'have the autonomy to exercise discretion in applying it to the infinitely varying individuals and circumstances' in society (Chubb and Moe, 1990, p.36).

Second, 'virtually everything about good education – from the knowledge and talents necessary to produce it to what it looks like when it is produced – defies formal measurement through the standardised categories of bureaucracy' (p.189). But bureaucracies need indicators of performance, and are likely to focus on factors which are objectively measurable – test scores, truancy rates, teacher qualifications – but which do not capture what is important about the educational process. They are likely then to make decisions and policy prescriptions based on these inadequate or misleading indicators.

Critically, bureaucratic control with 'its clumsy efforts to measure the unmeasurable' (p.189) are simply *not necessary* because, *third*, schools must please their clients, and to accomplish this, teachers

'need to perform as effectively as possible – which induces them ... to favor decentralized forms of organization that take full advantage of professionalism, discretionary judgement, informal cooperation and teams' (pp.189-90).

Fourth, and finally, good education must be focused on individual needs. But administrators cannot know the students as individuals: 'Bureaucracy inherently requires equal treatment for people who are in fact very different' (p.37). But parents and schools can recognise and respond to those differences – as long as they are not constrained by bureaucracy.

76

Now, those in favour of a compulsory curriculum and in favour of compulsory schooling would be forced to argue the opposite to each of these statements – that decisions about education should be made at the national level, that the locus of decision-making should be moved from the sphere of, say, families[2] to central government. The assumption seems to be that this will not only bring the benefits of national control, but also that there are no costs in changing the locus of control. However, it is crucial to the argument here that decision-making by government is not costless in this way. When decisions are moved between different levels of decision-making, it is not simply the case that a different set of people now make the decisions, but that *the nature of the decision itself can change* (Sowell, 1980, p.17).

To put this into more concrete form, we can consider a further example from the imposition of the National Curriculum in England and Wales. One of the National Curriculum's avowed aims was that there should be a 'broad and balanced' curriculum. So primary schools were encouraged to ensure that every child had access to a curriculum of science, history, geography, and lots of other good things. An early survey of reading in primary schools found standards falling, and it was suggested the connection between this and the state imposed crowding of the primary curriculum with broad and balanced fare, leading to little time on basic literacy and numeracy (Cato and Whetton, 1991).

So the desire for a broad and balanced primary curriculum – a notion which was uncontroversial at the time, indeed, widely applauded by left and right – may have led to a decline in reading standards. A recent report says that a whole cohort of youngsters is suffering educationally because of this lack of attention to basic literacy and numeracy (*The Times*, 28 November 1995). This example provides a useful way of seeing the dangers of state intervention in the curriculum. The important differences between a national curriculum and a 'market-led' curriculum are in terms of the ease of reversibility of decisions; the possibility of incremental changes; and the ease of fine tuning.

---

[2] Throughout, 'family' means any voluntary child-rearing arrangement, not necessarily the 'nuclear' family.

If an individual school had experimented with the broadening of its curriculum in this way, then upon discovery of a decline in reading standards, the solution would be obvious and quickly initiated. Teachers working with students would be able to give immediate feedback of problems encountered, and the decision could be reversed well before a whole cohort of pupils had gone through the year. With the experiment conducted at the national level, however, things become extraordinarily complicated, expensive and slow to change. For the curriculum is now on the statute book, brought there by lengthy and slow procedures, with its own interest groups which have fought long and hard for it, and only possible to be changed via similarly lengthy and slow procedures. In the example of England and Wales, the process took six years – and still there is no guarantee that the revised curriculum will have solved this problem, or indeed, what other unforeseen problems it may have introduced.

Moreover, this underestimates the complexity of the problem of feedback more generally. Feedback on the effectiveness of the compulsory curriculum could be obtained by, for example, results in reading tests. Bureaucratic control needs tangible results such as this by which to monitor whether national goals are being met, and whether the structure of the curriculum needs to be changed. Even with something as simple and presumably as objective as reading, it is surprising how difficult it has been for assessment boards to reach conclusions on valid and reliable methods for measuring these – and the political fall-out that has resulted from the ensuing tests, including strikes by the major teaching unions. How much more difficult, both in principle and in practice, it would be to suggest what objective and quantifiable measures could be used to ascertain whether *education* more broadly is taking place, particularly an education for something as intangible as Barber's 'sustenance' of the planet, or White's 'education for autonomy'.

Central planners will need to have some feedback, and hence they are likely to come up with measures which do not really reflect what is important about this education. They are likely to dwell on things that can be easily quantified, such as test scores, and truancy rates, rather than on less tangible aspects of the educational experience. This is not true, of course, of decision-makers at school level. They are continually interacting with pupils and aware of the multiplicity of their educational experiences. They are in a much better position to evaluate any changes, even if they are not able to articulate this evaluation to the degree required by state educational administrators.

Incremental Changes and Innovation

The change in locus of decision-making also changes the ease with which incremental changes can be made; this in turn affects the ease with which innovation can be introduced. Decisions that are reversible are also flexible, allowing for innovations to be introduced and tried out, and perhaps rejected or more widely disseminated. Government-made decisions are much more likely not to foster innovations in this way. Consider the reading standards example. If a school discovers this decline, then it could, as noted above, quickly reverse the previous decision, and eliminate (say) science, from the first years of schooling. However, it does not have to do that. It is more likely to make incremental changes, by raising the level of time devoted to science, but not by as much as before. Or it could introduce the innovation of a longer teaching week, allowing more time for science *and* reading. But importantly, these changes could be introduced in a spirit of 'we'll try this and see what happens'. If it is not successful, if reading standards continue to decline, or if children or parents or staff object to the longer hours, then the decisions can again be adjusted until the outcome is as desired.

Governments, however, cannot continue to make incremental changes and innovations in this way. Even if the necessary feedback mechanisms could be put in place, it would be politically inexpedient for democratic governments to persist in introducing incremental changes. Again we have the experience with the National Curriculum in England and Wales to learn from. A spate of incremental changes has led to the promise of a moratorium on any changes for five years. So if there are any other unforeseen problems, or if the curriculum is still not resolved to people's satisfaction, or even if changing circumstances require changing curricula, it *cannot* be changed for another five years.

Fine Tuning

Finally, another facet of decision-making relationships of relevance to the curriculum relates to the ease with which decisions can be fine tuned to the particular problem at hand.

79

Teachers in schools have continual feedback from their students, and are thus able to assess the effectiveness of the curriculum for *individuals,* and gauge work accordingly. The central planners are clearly not able to fine tune the curriculum to suit the needs of individuals in this way.

One way around this would be to leave the broad framework of the curriculum to the central planners, and allow teachers discretion in the classroom. This is certainly how some central curriculum planners view their work. White, for example, envisages that his curriculum will overcome the types of problems discussed in this section:

> '[I]t is essential for teaching to be adapted to the needs and strengths of the learner. ... a teacher ... knows the particular circumstances in which learning takes place ... Effective teaching requires the freedom to make specific planning decisions in response to such factors. The national framework should support teachers in such planning, not constrain them unduly.' (O'Hear and White, 1991, p.10)

Barber views his outline in the same way (Barber, 1994). However, it has already been suggested how the problem of competing visions will lead to national curricula being highly prescriptive, and not likely to leave areas of the curriculum to the discretion of teachers.

What fine tuning could take place in a curriculum not nationally imposed, in the reading standards example? Clearly, teachers could encourage those who *are* able to read to cover areas of science, while allowing those who are not to spend time in mastery of reading. The solution is simple, but the inflexibility of a national curriculum is likely to undermine it. Centrally imposed decisions are likely to be package deals rather than individualised. Again, this is precisely what has happened with the National Curriculum in England and Wales. It is (proudly) claimed to be 'an entitlement' curriculum; it is presumably of little comfort to those who are finding it hard to read to know that they are benefiting from such an entitlement.

If the curriculum needs to be flexible, fostering innovation and allowing for incremental changes and fine tuning to cater for the needs of individuals, then the knowledge requirements for the curriculum will not be found at the national level. It is the rich fund of individual knowledge, sometimes tacit and unarticulable, which Hayek pointed to, that is needed in making decisions about curricula. Crucially, this knowledge is not accessible to the national planners. The example given of the inflexibility of the National Curriculum in England and Wales shows how the epistemic argument is not an abstract concern, but reveals problems which may have blighted the early education of many young people today.

But there is a further aspect to the difficulty of central planning of the curriculum, which is simply to do with the immensity of what is required: this is not central planning of how to mine coal, or how to run a railway industry, for example, complex as these might be. It is central planning of *the prerequisites for living the good life*. For that is what the educational curriculum is – and educationalists such as Barber are proud of the significance of their work for the human condition. But does not this bring home the haughtiness of those who suggest that they, with their committees, will be able to decide what is best for people, to enable them to live this good life? How can they be so sure that their ideas will enable the good life to be lived? Are they sure they have taken everything into account?

Barber, for example, read history at Oxford, and so perhaps this part of his curriculum vision will have been carefully thought through – although even then, of course, one can wonder whether he really has taken into account all the opposing viewpoints. But what about the other aspects of the curriculum? Presumably he will bring in others to define the details of the core skills, the mathematics and science curricula, and so on, but bringing in committees of people does not solve the problem at all.

A first problem concerns who would be on the many committees and subcommittees. For we can guess that the choice of those people could largely determine the result of the deliberations. Will there be people who largely agree on political issues, or will there be a balance of political colour, and hence great difficulties in reaching agreement? But greater difficulty in reaching agreement, as we noted above, is likely to lead to excessively detailed legislation, a far cry from the curriculum guidelines which Barber envisages.

Even if the knowledge, or some part of it, can be articulated *within separate disciplines*,[3] will the experts from these

---

[3] Note that there is a long tradition in political philosophy which queries whether much knowledge about society is of this articulated form, or

different fields be able to communicate with each other, and understand each other in order to create a coherent curriculum? For the great expansion of knowledge means that there can no longer be a 'Renaissance Person', familiar with all fields. As Hayek wrote:

> 'The more civilised we become the more relatively ignorant must each individual be of the facts on which the working of his civilisation depends. The very division of knowledge increases the necessary ignorance of the individual of most of this knowledge.' (Hayek, 1960, p.26)

This has profound implications for any central curriculum planners, who will be largely ignorant of all but, presumably, a subset of one of the disciplines brought to bear on the planning, such as economics, history, curriculum subjects, philosophy, psychology, politics, etc. How will Barber's committees communicate with each other, and balance their different claims?

Finally, even if it is assumed that the central planners can put forward a plausible articulation of their ideas, and even if this could be comprehensible across different disciplines, can we be sure that they have not overlooked any unintended consequences that may undermine the policy? The decline in reading standards example is just one of many that could be given. The general point is that, given the complexity of our social system, we simply cannot be sure how different aspects interrelate, and how changes in one area will affect other areas and institutions: the necessary knowledge is dispersed amongst those who would be making decisions in the curriculum market-place.

The upshot of all this is that there are severe knowledge problems facing the central curriculum planners, analogous to the problems facing any other central planning. The knowledge argument and the problem of competing visions severely undermine any desire to impose a national curriculum on educational settings. Even an outline as seemingly innocuous as Barber's would open up all the problems outlined here. Each unique individual holds different knowledge and skills, and has different educational

---

whether it is knowledge that is 'tacit', discovered only through practices and traditions (see, for example, Hayek, 1960, Oakeshott, 1962, Polanyi, 1958).

requirements; information concerning this distribution of knowledge and skills could never be known by any central planning authority. This brings us back to the arguments which raised this discussion about the curriculum in the first place.

A Market-led Curriculum

The argument in this chapter is that in both places where the curriculum arose as an issue in our discussion of markets, to suppose that there is a justification for government regulation of the curriculum would be mistaken. *First*, in the thought experiment it was suggested that families might not know best about the curriculum requirements of their children; and judgement was suspended about whether this would leave a place for state intervention in the curriculum. It is now argued that the 'knowledge argument' above suggests that families are much more likely to know more of what is relevant for their children's education than any state curriculum council could:

> '[P]ublic authorities cannot possibly have access to the same kind of detailed knowledge of family circumstances and desires that the families themselves have' (Peacock and Wiseman, 1964, p.20).

Hence the optimistic conclusions concerning markets from Chapter 2 are upheld, and the only state intervention in education that is required is the minimal funding for the poor and selective compulsion for those not partaking of educational opportunities.

Second, when the demands of equality or equity were examined, it was suggested that the notion of an 'adequate' education might lead to government intervention in the curriculum being sought to ensure this, in part for its value as an information indicator to parents and students. Now we have suggested that the problems of competing visions and the knowledge problem are far more likely to lead to difficulties with seeking government intervention in this way; difficulties which would lead to the undermining of the adequacy of educational opportunities delivered through a government compulsory curriculum. Again we can conclude that an adequate education is more likely to be obtained by leaving the curriculum to demand expressed through markets.

There will be resistance to this conclusion from some quarters. Surely it cannot be argued, to put the matter in terms of Barr's question raised at the end of the last chapter, that *all* parents would make better decisions than a government taking decisions *in loco parentis*? In the thought experiment of Chapter 2 (backed up by historical evidence in Chapter 3), we did point to the small number of parents who would not allow their children educational opportunities, and suggested that 'selective compulsion' might be needed in such circumstances. Similarly, it might be thought that the educational settings attended by these children would also need to have prescribed curricula, as the parents are likely to be ill-informed. But here the power of the market emerges again. For these children will be compelled, and funded if necessary, to attend educational settings *which are part of* the mainstream educational opportunities available, and hence will have curricula which concerned parents are monitoring. Markets do not need *everyone* to be informed, in order for high quality to be ensured.

Barr puts the matter in the form of a moral and, for him, perplexing question:

> '[I]f the quality of parental choice varies systematically with socioeconomic status, how do we weigh the relative claims of middle-class children and their parents to be allowed private choice, against those of children in lower socioeconomic groups, whose interests might be served better by the state?' (Barr, 1993, p.349)

Ignoring the questionable assumption that the lower socio-economic groups would *necessarily* be ill-informed, we can put the question in the context of the discussion here, and find the answer is easy. *All* should be allowed to exercise choice. For if all have access to the 'one-tier' market system, then the choices of those who are better informed will help raise the quality of the choices of all. Indeed, this is precisely the argument that is raised for encouraging middle-class parents to remain within the state system, rather than opt out to private schools, that they will help raise standards for all. That argument has the weakness that the politically inarticulate, those not good at using the 'voice'[4] option, have to

---

[4] Hirschman (1970) showed how the management of an organisation can discover that its customers are dissatisfied with its performance in one of

rely entirely on the politically adept to raise standards, which has not been noticeably successful for the less advantaged. The educational markets in our thought experiment capitalise on the power of common access, so that the better informed keep standards high, while simultaneously giving the additional power of 'exit' to all, which in itself is a powerful mechanism for raising standards.

Indeed, this discussion has implications for the discussion of political equality, mentioned in passing in Chapter 4. White (1990), for example, sought political equality to ensure that all have control over the curriculum, not just a privileged group – professional educationalists and politicians. It seems highly unlikely that democratic control could achieve this, for the reasons outlined above. It is committed interest groups which are likely to decide the curriculum, if even a democratic state has control, not the people as a whole. But notice how powerful the thought experiment market model of Chapter 2 seems in this respect. For in the market, all the ordinary people that White would want to be, *are* 'in control' of the curriculum. The professional educationalists and curriculum visionaries can still set their curricular agendas, in conjunction with the media, business and industry, and so on. But parents and children can decide which of these to patronise, and the market mechanisms would allow those that parents and children favoured to be more successful than those they rejected. In this way power is dispersed to all, not just to a select group.

Another very important factor emerges here. Those who argue for political equality are likely to be most concerned that the *disadvantaged* have a greater say than they otherwise would in the decision-making process. In current political systems, this is fulfilled only imperfectly, in that everyone (more or less) has the vote, but some have a considerably greater say than others. But in the thought experiment market, because of the funding safety net, the

---

two ways, through 'exit', where the customers stop buying the good, or through 'voice', where customers express their dissatisfaction by complaining to management or some other authority. State intervention in education leads to the primacy of the voice option, which is likely to be best utilised by the 'politically influential, skilled and adroit' middle-classes (Seldon, 1990). Markets lead to the exit option being available (as well as voice), which can benefit all.

most disadvantaged are guaranteed an influence on educational provision. For they, as much as anyone else, have the right of 'exit' in the educational market-place, and it is this mechanism that will help to ensure quality provision for those students. Educational establishments that fail to attract enough pupils would be closed, hence there is always an incentive for such establishments to ensure that they *do* attract and keep students.

Moreover, the power the funding voucher[5] gives the disadvantaged is likely to be greater than the power the democratic process gives them. The disadvantaged are in a small minority, and on their own they are not able to influence policy significantly through voting, for they are a minority unlikely to be organised and unlikely to be able to enter into coalitions with others. Hence they are not able to campaign for improvements to their educational opportunities, and would have to rely on altruistic others to do this for them. But in our market model, each of them carries the threat of withdrawing the funding voucher from any educational institution which fails to provide them with quality service. Each of them has access to the market mechanism which can improve quality.

We have arrived at a vindication of markets – with a minimum safety net – in education. These markets will satisfy demands for equality or equity; they have been shown to be historically viable; they do not require detailed state regulation; and they can satisfy the desire for democratic accountability. Chapter 6 suggests some policy proposals which would begin to turn this vision into reality.

---

[5] The final chapter suggests a form which this voucher might take.

6 | Towards Education Without the State: The Learning Society and the Market

Thomas Sowell once observed that there are better automobiles in the ghettos than schools. But it is not just cars: there are better shops, supermarkets, banks, amusement arcades, fast-food stores and virtually every other private service you can think of. Where I have lived in Brixton, for example, is one of the poorer areas of London; nearby a new supermarket has recently opened. It is as fine as any supermarket anywhere. It has the same fine selection of goods, standards of cleanliness, and innovative technology – technology that would have been unheard of even 10 years ago. Compare the supermarket with the local secondary school. This has dilapidated buildings and uncared for grounds; it is an unpleasant place to be for teachers and pupils alike. Perhaps most significantly, unlike the supermarket, in the school the technology is virtually the same as it was when the school was first opened 100 years ago: one teacher to a large class of children.

If markets deliver goods and services better in other areas of our lives, why not in education? The answer has always been that there are justifications for state intervention in education which show why governments need to override markets. This paper has investigated the most important justifications and found them wanting.

One justification was that, without the state, there would not be sufficient educational opportunities; the historical evidence of a functioning market in education, as well as more recent evidence, undermined this proposition. Another important justification was that markets in education would exacerbate inequality and be intolerably unfair or inequitable. However, state education has also suffered from inequality and unfairness. Moreover, when we examined what is meant by equity (and why equality was desirable) it appeared that markets (with a safety net) could satisfy this: they could ensure adequate educational opportunities for all, and could also satisfy demands for political equality. Finally, the notion that there needs to be state control of the curriculum was explored. This was shown to come up against severe difficulties, including the crucial 'knowledge' problem.

Thus far, it has been suggested that fears of moving towards markets in education, toward privatisation of schooling, would not be justified. Now it is time to return to the existing reality of state education. We have suggested that having no government intervention in terms of provision of education, none in terms of regulation, over and above what would be normally required for business to operate in a market, and no funding, would be desirable. The two exceptions to this would be for the poor, who would require some funding, and the educationally irresponsible, who would be subject to some compulsion.

However, we could not move overnight to such a state of affairs. It would be extraordinarily difficult to persuade people that government was not needed in education, and extraordinarily difficult, too, to persuade politicians that education was an area in which their control could be relinquished. Indeed, the more governments seem willing to countenance a reduced rôle in some economic areas, the more they hold on to education as being a key area for their continued intervention. This chapter explores some small-scale reforms which could move state education systems towards markets.[1]

The proposals suggested are modest, and will not satisfy libertarian purists. However, they have the merit that, while they are definitely steps towards a genuine market in education, they could also be considered as desirable reforms in their own right, whatever the final goal sought.[2] The proposed reforms seek to liberate the supply and demand

---

[1] The aim is not to provide a detailed blueprint for arriving at markets in education. To attempt this would be foolish, given how entrenched is state intervention. The aim is to sketch out the first steps in bringing market mechanisms to bear; the degree to which these steps take purchase will define the later steps in the process.

[2] Stuart Sexton, one of the architects of Local Management of Schools in England and Wales, pointed out how this reform was so succesful because it brought about something which was found to be desirable by schools, whatever they thought of its ultimate aim as a step towards markets in education (personal communication).

sides of education further, and to bring in elements of pricing mechanisms. But the proposals will not go as far as we have gone in our counterfactual and philosophical discussions. They take for granted what for many is an unquestionable position, that the state has an important rôle in the finance of education. Accepting this as a necessary short- to medium-term constraint, we will examine what market mechanisms can be brought in to enhance the quality of education within this limitation.

Was the preceding discussion necessary, then, if the proposals here are to be more modest? I think so. For objections to the moves considered here, towards more genuine markets in education, will meet with resistance. This resistance is often expressed in terms of an apprehension of where the reforms are leading: this paper has shown that if a genuine market in education *is* the ultimate goal, then it is not to be feared.

The proposals are genuine steps towards privatisation, in that they all lead to the bringing back, slowly but surely, of market incentives into schooling. They promote an atmosphere where the educational development of the customer[3] is of paramount importance, the needs of the suppliers less so. But also, they fit into the context of the growing discussion of the need for a 'learning society', discussion becoming increasingly widespread in academic, business and government circles. The proposals here break the hold of government on this initiative, and show how strengthening market mechanisms can better enhance it.

Recent Reform in England and Wales

In this chapter, my proposals are put into the context of England and Wales, building on educational reforms of the last decade. The measures, however, will be applicable, with appropriate modifications, to education systems elsewhere. Nations – or policy-makers and educationalists within nations

---

[3] Who is the customer? The parent or, for older 'children', the young person him or herself. Some query this use of language, saying that there are other 'customers' of education, pointing to employers and other citizens. This seems to be obscurantism. Yes, employers and fellow citizens have an interest in having children well educated; but so do they have an interest in having children well fed: does this make employers and fellow citizens customers of children's food too?

– are learning from one another; it is worth pointing out the features of current educational reform in England and Wales, illustrating those aspects which are conducive to markets, and those which inhibit them. For there is much to praise in recent reforms, as well as many pitfalls to avoid.

The current reforms can best be understood as being on two levels, the decentralising and the centralising.[4] The key decentralising measures are Local Management of Schools (LMS), Grant Maintained (GM) schools, *per capita* funding and open enrolment.

Under LMS, funds were devolved to schools from the Local Education Authorities, which previously decided all of each school's financial affairs. Presently, 85 per cent of funds must be devolved to schools, although some authorities allocate more, and there is discussion about increasing the compulsory level to 95 per cent. Although widely resisted on its introduction, local management has been immensely successful. Instead of being forced to use local authority services, whatever their quality and without any control over their cost, schools can now shop around for the best and most cost-effective service available. It makes no sense, as one high-ranking teacher union official recently told me, not to allow schools to have this large degree of autonomy over their own budgets. Grant maintained schools extend this principle, allowing schools to 'opt out' of the local authority altogether, and receive their funds directly from central government. Thus they are completely in charge of all their current expenditure, and are able to use funds as they wish for innovative purposes.

Per capita funding means that money is allocated to schools on the basis of the number of children enrolled, so, to some extent, funds 'follow children', albeit clumsily. In this way, schools are, to a degree, financially sensitive to how many pupils they can attract, or that they are losing. Finally, open enrolment obliges schools to accept students up to a calculated 'standard number', allowing parental choice to be expressed, at least to some degree. Certainly it avoids the situation which

---

4   Students of government can observe how the decentralising measures came with deliberate *quid pro quo* centralising measures (see Ball, 1990c). Power was devolved to the people, but then extra powers were taken to ensure that people did not abuse the power given to them.

used to happen where students were not granted their desire to go to a popular school, even though there were places available, but were redirected to a less popular school, in order to balance the numbers in each.

In tandem with these reforms, however, the government introduced quite extensive 'centralising' measures. These include the National Curriculum, national testing, and compulsory league tables. The National Curriculum gave detailed prescription of all subjects to be taught throughout schools, with each subject forced into the same 10-level, four-key stage mould. National testing was prescribed at ages 7, 11, 14 and 16, and the results at 16 and probably 11 are recorded in national league tables, together with truancy levels and other indicators.

The 'decentralising' reforms are to be applauded; the proposals suggested here build upon and extend these measures. The 'centralising' reforms, however, are not desirable in terms of moves towards markets; the proposals here show how they can be undermined.

Liberation of Demand

Key Problems

The key problems inhibiting the expression of educational demand are fourfold.

- *First*, parents and young people are not, in general, aware of their own buying power.

- *Second*, demand, by law, can only be expressed at a particular time in a child's or young person's life, namely between the ages of five and 16.[5] But many people wish to partake of learning opportunities later in life, while many *do not* wish to do so in their early teens.

- *Third*, the state dictates that a certain amount of money is used for schooling – currently roughly £2,000 per child per year, excluding capital costs. Schools are guaranteed this money per child (and much more for special needs and disadvantaged children), and so have no incentives to look

---

[5] A largely middle-class minority, of course, is able to express state-funded demand for five or more years longer than that.

for efficiency improvements which could deliver comparable or better services below this price.[6]

- *Fourth*, parents and young people are unable to use any of their own funds on schooling (although they are, of course, able to use funds on other educational activities) unless they have the considerable funds needed for private schooling. Moreover, we have noted that we are working within the constraints of a state-funded system – but even so it might be wondered whether the state has to fund *all* of the schooling costs, or whether huge incentives to ensure that money is spent wisely and effectively could be created if *some part* of the funds was paid for by parents or young people.

My proposal to liberate the demand side tackles all of these issues.

Those in favour of markets in education normally argue for 'vouchers' as a way forward. (For a particularly excellent summary of the issues, see Seldon, 1986.) My argument builds on that work, but puts it into the context of current debates about the 'learning society' and learning credits.

Towards the Learning Society

The Commission on Social Justice (1994), set up by the late John Smith to transform Labour Party fortunes, proposed a 'Learning Bank' and an Individual Learning Account, 'which enables everybody to have access to lifelong learning' (p.141), that is, access to 'the learning society'. The National Commission on Education (1995) supported this notion, which enables government, individuals and employers to contribute to a fund for learning. The Government, in its consultation document *Lifetime Learning* (DFEE, 1995), has also recommended that 'voluntary individual savings accounts' are explored as one possible way forward to address this issue.

Many of these ideas are to be applauded. Indeed, the Commission on Social Justice espouses sentiments which could almost serve as a motto for this chapter: The Individual Learning Account 'would allow individuals to learn *when*

---

[6] Recall how in the thought experiment in Chapter 2 we showed how financial problems led to entrepreneurs being able to offer comparable or better services at a lower price.

appropriate to them, and in the *form* appropriate to them' (Commission on Social Justice, 1994, p.143). Genuine expression of demand and consumer responsiveness are key areas which the market model aims to enhance. Unfortunately, the Commission on Social Justice then went on to dictate what these genuine expressions and responses should be, rather than trusting the relationship between buyer and seller to *discover* what they are in the market-place.

I am going to steal their clothes, but alter them to my own ends, integrating the pressures for a 'learning society' with my market reforms. The key problem with all of these proposals is that no-one has been bold enough to ask why there is the bifurcation between compulsory schooling up to the age of 16 years, and 'life-long learning' post-16. For there seems to be nothing in the arguments for the 'learning society' which would support such a distinction. Getting rid of it is the key to progress towards the learning society, and, as it happens, towards markets in education.

The notion of a 'learning society' needs some explication: the consensus is that we are in a period of rapid technological and social change, change which will continue to accelerate. The learning society is variously seen as a coping strategy for society and individuals for this rapid change. Husén (1974, p.24), for example, argued that 'it simply will not do to prepare for the whole life we shall have inside and outside the job world' in formal schooling. Similarly, Ball (1993, p.7) notes: 'The world changes too fast for our initial education and training to prove adequate for an adult lifetime'. Moreover, embracing the learning society is seen by many as the only way in which a national economy can survive, or compete. Drucker (1993) points to 'productivity of knowledge' as being the

'determining factor in the competitive position of a country, an industry, a company. ... The only thing that increasingly will matter in national as well as in international economics is management's performance in making knowledge productive' (p.176).

Indeed, ideas on the learning society go further than these – it is seen as enhancing social cohesiveness (Drucker, 1993, p.187) and empowering communities (Ranson, 1992, p.71).

Finally, and of relevance given our discussion in Chapter 4, the learning society is seen as an important way of improving equity: because it provides individuals with 'second-chance' learning opportunities, it enables those who fail, or do not wish to make use of opportunities, at school to have further opportunities later in life. For example, Husén (1974) writes that

> 'a person should not miss out on the chance to benefit from quality education if he did not receive it, or did not care for it, when he was young' (p.24).

Why are individuals not partaking of life-long learning opportunities? There would seem to be three reasons. *First*, motivational reasons, ranging from a lack of confidence in themselves as learners, because of unpleasant experiences of schooling, to disillusion with learning as simply being 'chasing paper qualifications'. *Second*, informational reasons, a lack of awareness of opportunities which are available. *Third*, there is a problem of lack of funds or inability to bear opportunity costs.

The proposed demand-side reform could help undermine all three of these reasons and hence make the learning society a reality, *and* liberate educational demand, *and* bring in a pricing mechanism, *and* start to undermine the ghettoisation of youth ... all in one modest proposal. Moreover, and crucially, the proposal would hardly cost anything in new government funds, a distinct advantage over all other proposals I have seen.

The Lifelong Individual Fund for Education

The key would be to lower the school-leaving age to, let us say, 14 years of age. Simultaneously, young people would be given, over a two-year period, funds equivalent to two years current account spending on schooling – around £4,000 (more for those with special needs) – which would be invested in their (let us call it) Lifelong Individual Fund for Education (LIFE).[7]

---

[7] A modification to this proposal would be to incorporate capital funds too, if the difficulties with ascertaining what these amount to could be worked out and agreed upon (see Davis, 1993, pp.34-36); it would also probably be politically desirable to move towards a national funding formula, to ensure that there are no accusations of regional unfairness in the system.

LIFEs could be opened at any time, and supplemented with additional funds at any time, by parents, grandparents, and young people themselves. They would be an obvious channel for philanthropy. Just as there are 'big brother/sister' schemes operating in several countries where a person adopts a disadvantaged youngster and helps him or her throughout life, so the opening of a LIFE account for someone could become a normal part of that process. Individuals and businesses and trusts could open or add to these accounts. The mentoring rôle would be enhanced as disadvantaged children are advised on when and how to use these funds most effectively. It would be philanthropy directed at enhancing individuals' lives, targeted to their individual needs and preferences. The accounts would not incur tax, and if possible (the Exchequer permitting) contributions to LIFE accounts would be tax deductible.

If an individual does not have an account by the time he or she reaches the age of 14, the government will open one for him or her. In either case, the government will add the appropriate funds to the accounts at that age. The LIFEs would be managed and invested by commercial banks if possible, or, in the unlikely event that none is interested, by a public company similar to that administering student loans, designed to move towards privatisation at the earliest convenience.

The funds, accruing interest and dividends, could be drawn upon at any time during a person's lifetime, with the stipulation that they can only be used either at approved educational settings (we will say what will satisfy this stipulation below), or that some proportion of them could be used for purchasing educational equipment such as a multimedia computer.[8]

One minor problem would be what to do concerning young people who are already in private schooling: Will they qualify for the state investment in their LIFE accounts? If so, this would mean extra expenditure for the Exchequer. However,

---

[8] There may be safeguards to ensure that this proportion is not abused: for example, £500 could be allocated to this, on the assumption that it would have to be supplemented by other funds to purchase a computer. If it was felt to be impossible to police this arrangement, then this suggestion could be dropped.

the extra amount would be small. About 50,000 young people would become eligible for the funds each year and, once the process was in operation, this would bring in the need for roughly £200 million to provide these young people with the same opportunities. There would seem to be an obvious way forward: make LIFE accounts available initially only to those who have been at a state secondary school from the age of 11 or 12 (to allow for middle schools). But phase in making these accounts available to all, over a period of, say, five years.

The main sources of finance for the extra funds required would be threefold. *First*, and providing the bulk of the funds, the Assisted Places Scheme would be phased out. Many would query this source of finance, particularly from a market-oriented perspective (see, for example, Flew, 1995). However, I am not in general in favour of the Assisted Places Scheme. It allows only a small minority to attend private schools who otherwise would not be able to; it is open to the objection that it perpetuates a 'two-tier' system, and exacerbates inequity. Indeed, it gives precisely to those who are doing well in the education system, allowing them an extra boost. But these young people are not necessarily the ones who need help *from the state*. Not a two-tier, but a '*one-tier*' system is what is needed, where everyone has the benefits of an education improved through authentic market incentives. The Assisted Places Scheme is thus an anachronism, and phasing it out in order to reap the wider benefits of markets for everyone should be welcomed. Or to look at it another way, *the proposals here bring the benefits of the Assisted Places Scheme to all*.

A *second* source of finance would be savings from post-16 education, for reasons given below. *Third*, there are likely to be savings as expensive surplus places within the state sector are closed – for the market will take up the slack which is currently a burden on the state system.

In parallel with the lowering of the compulsory schooling age, regulations concerning working hours for young people could also be modified, to allow some who leave school early to work if they wish.[9] Finally, if it was possible for government to move towards considerably lower taxes, so that families had

---

[9] Interestingly, the minimum age at which it is lawful for children to be employed is still 13 years, under the Children's Act 1972, s.1.

more funds to dispose of as they see fit, the value of the government contribution to the LIFE account could be fixed, or even progressively lowered. As time goes on, in the context of a lower tax régime, voluntary contributions to the account could become an increasing proportion of the funds available. For richer people, eventually, the government contribution could be phased out altogether; for poorer people, there could always be a government contribution.[10]

Some Examples

What would happen to some typical young people under this proposal? Consider three, Emma, Jayshree and Phil, all, let us say, from working-class backgrounds and none with wealthy parents, in order to emphasise the advantages of the system to the less advantaged. Moreover, it will not be assumed that any of these three have extra funds in their accounts from other sources – changing the examples to allow for this would make the proposal even more attractive.

First, Emma, a young person, doing well at academic subjects at school, assumed by her teachers to be heading for university. When the proposal is first brought into being, someone in her position probably would continue in school. She would use her LIFE funds to pay for two years of schooling in the normal way, before continuing to do her 'A' levels, and then on to university. But, as the new freedom and incentives created by the fund are begun to be realised, different approaches might be considered.[11] For example, the academic young person might wonder why it is taking so long to study for her school-leaving examinations: perhaps the

---

[10] Eventually, once the system had been shown to be working, the government contribution could become a loan on future earnings – a modified income-contingent loan collected through the tax or National Insurance system – with preferential interest rates. This would enable the vast majority of people to become more or less completely independent of state funding (see West, 1975).

[11] At all stages in this chapter, I must stress that, unlike others who propose educational reform, I am not pointing to specific things that *must* happen, but merely suggesting how there will be improved incentives to allow for innovation. If people are perfectly happy with the *status quo*, then the *status quo* would continue. It is only if they are dissatisfied that change will occur.

work has simply expanded to fit the available – and compulsory – time-period?[12]

It is also the experience of many teachers and students that things are taught over and over again in schools – secondary schools repeat material that has been learnt in primary schools; later secondary school repeats what has been learnt in the early years of secondary school, and so on. Given the choice of going through their exam syllabus at a leisurely pace over five years, or going faster over three or four years and leaving school to do something else, many young people might consider the latter a preferable option. So it may well be that *market* pressure would be brought on schools to allow for some speeding up of the process for those children who think that they can move faster. Some children might be able to save all of the £4,000 in their LIFE by doing their examinations early, others a large proportion of the funds; these could then be used for other educational opportunities later, including university education, or whatever. Or some proportion could be used for buying a CD-ROM multimedia system to help them with their studies.

What would Emma do then, upon leaving school early? Perhaps she will do 'A' levels earlier; or she might take a year or two out to be a community service volunteer, or to develop artistic or musical talents, or run a small business, or teach younger children, or obtain (genuine) work experience, or whatever. All worthwhile activities, and for those that seek them, preferable to slowly moving through schooling at a pace dictated not by their needs, but by the requirements of the system.

Next, Jayshree. She is less good at academic subjects, better at some practical subjects, but overall not sure what she wishes do with her life. Again, if she wants to, she can just carry on as normal, authorising the payment of school fees from her LIFE to her school, following the National Curriculum towards her school-leaving examinations. But alternatively, if she is dissatisfied with this, she can consider

---

[12] I taught in Zimbabwe, for example, where Cambridge 'O' levels were taken after four years of secondary education, to no apparent defect. Indeed, the percentage pass rate for 'O' levels in Zimbabwe as a whole was about the same as for England and Wales, and this was with examinations taken in a second language, with poor educational resources, as well as only the four years of secondary schooling!

other options (and of course these options are also available to Emma if she wants).

The new flexibility would enable Jayshree to think of her own particular values, skills and interests. Perhaps her interest in practical or artistic subjects means she should concentrate on these, and she can explore places other than school for pursuing them. Or perhaps she might muse whether it is her *particular* school which has not allowed her to develop academically, and that other places might better help her in that way. So she can shop around for opportunities that better suit her personal values, attitudes and requirements. Or she might decide that she wants to be 'out of education' for now, and into work, or travel, and feel happy that she can do this and still have funds to be used at a later stage, when she is feeling more ready to consider what she wants to do. Or she could consider a combination of these, for her LIFE is flexible: she could pay an approved mathematics tutor, work part-time, and attend technology courses at a private college. The world really is her oyster.

Again, this would encourage educational suppliers, including innovative state schools, to think more creatively about what they can offer. Just as we do not have to shop all year around at Sainsbury's, just because we once shopped there, so there is nothing to suggest that education is best obtained if the person attends only one school for all of the time. Some schools might consider contracting out services to a variety of suppliers, and then sell the whole package to young people. Or other educational agencies might emerge which create such flexible packages.

Moreover, another important pressure will begin to work on schools. For, even if Jayshree decides that school is the best place for her, she would obviously prefer to save some of her funds if possible, to use for further education and training later in life, or to buy a notebook computer. An innovative school might look for ways to cut costs, so that it could attract Jayshree with lower fees, while still delivering a high-quality education. (This is one crucial way in which LIFE accounts are preferable to voucher systems, at least in the short term; the latter always guarantee schools a certain amount of money, so therefore do not give them strong incentives to explore cheaper alternatives. LIFE accounts are completely flexible and so bring much more market pressure to bear on schools.)

For example, it was hinted in the thought experiment of Chapter 2 that one way for schools to cut costs might be to reconsider the staff-technology inputs into teaching, and also to consider using assistant teachers as well as more expensive trained teachers. If one school starts to experiment in this way, then, if it is successful, all schools will have to become similarly more cost-conscious. Pressures for innovation which are wholly absent from the state system now could be brought to bear, avoiding waste (if, of course, there is any in the system) and liberating funds for greater educational opportunity later in life. The market pressures could help make the learning society a reality.

Finally, what of Phil? He is a low-achieving young man, not good at academic subjects, nor practical ones. He hates school. His teachers predict that he will be one of the 10 per cent who leaves school without any qualifications at age 16. Now at age 14 he can simply leave the environment that he feels has done nothing for him. Here the power of the proposal really comes home. For, while in the current system he would leave school at 16 with nothing, and having used up all his state allocation of funds, now there is no such waste. He can leave school, with no qualifications, true, but still with two years' funds to take with him. He will be less frustrated, have less resentment to 'education' simply because he has had less time for it to build up.

What will he do next? I suppose he might hang around on street corners, get involved in crime, and so on. If so, that would at least be no worse than at present. But he now has £4,000 (at least – probably more from government if he is a special needs student, and still more if charities, companies or individuals have singled him out as being particularly deserving) in his LIFE account. He has time on his hands and is aware that educational entrepreneurs are eager for his money. Perhaps he will decide that he might as well use some of it now, perhaps on becoming literate or numerate, perhaps on attending a course which shows him how to run a small business, complete with start-up funds.[13] Perhaps after

---

[13] Along the lines of the courses run by BusinessWise in London, or the National Foundation for Teaching Entrepreneurship (NFTE) in the USA. These bodies are financed largely by charitable donations to cater for young people failed by the system; they could expand enormously if LIFE funds were available to them.

hanging around on street corners for a few months, without any compulsion to be anywhere, he might even find it desirable to go back to school, particularly if school realises it now has a real incentive to encourage him back.

This brings us to the final advantage of the system. For secondary schools can now cease to be 'ghettos' for young people aged 11-16 (or 18). Older people – anyone aged 16 or above – will also be encouraged back to school to learn alongside younger children. These could be older people without LIFE accounts initially, encouraged to attend lessons for their own intrinsic pleasure or for qualifications, as well as those returning after a couple of years using LIFE money. Several schools are already experimenting with this approach – and at present need to receive funds through a further education college. If this regulation was also waived, the system could be greatly enhanced.

These older people will provide valuable rôle models, if nothing else – for they will be able to advise young people on the opportunities in the real world, in a way in which teachers cannot. If schooling is worthwhile and leads to increased opportunities – which would be the only reason why the adults are there in the first place – then they could be drumming this home to young people who are not sure of the point of it at all.

LIFE funds could be contributed to by employers or government later in life, as the Commission on Social Justice suggests. Or other government initiatives, such as Career Development Loans (currently available from major banks with government paying the interest on the loan during the period of training), could be integrated into the arrangements for LIFE accounts, and other loan arrangements also incorporated. But that is as far as I wish to explore their use. The important point is that they dramatically liberate the educational demand side. They bring very important incentives into schooling, allow increased funds to be used, and used more efficiently, and facilitate the development of the learning society.

Once these ideas gain credence, they will be seen as more widely applicable. Even keeping compulsory schooling up to age 14, an obvious next step would be to introduce the funds to be used from age 11. Young people and parents will then have control over their LIFEs for all of their secondary schooling, and almost all of the market pressures I have

101

mentioned above will be brought to bear, ensuring flexibility to accommodate to individual needs and interests. And if at age 11, why not from the very beginning of schooling? The logic of the process seems unstoppable, if it was found to be working well for older children.

Liberation of the Supply Side

Building on Current Reform

The liberation of the supply side is of crucial importance if the educational market is to function well – and if the market is to overcome some of the problems of inequity, for example, which we discussed in Chapter 4. Again, in the context of reforms in England and Wales, many of the reforms do begin this process; the proposals here build on these. The importance of Local Management of Schools cannot be over-stressed. Moves to increase the proportion of the budget devolved to schools would be welcomed, which would make all schools increasingly able to behave with the freedom of grant-maintained schools. Of course, it would be desirable if all schools could become wholly autonomous, but there seem to be political objections to that. Certainly, schools should not be compelled to become grant-maintained, which would only exacerbate the objections to the market-style reforms. However, there are quite severe restrictions on the liberating of the supply side which government has imposed; these need to be addressed.

Before considering these, we examine the stipulation above that LIFE funds need to be used at 'approved' educational institutions or settings. What form will this take? It would be ideal if 'approved' status could be given to any educational setting which was able to register under the normal procedures for the registration of independent (private) schools. Here the procedure is fairly minimal, with schools required to lodge details such as intake numbers, examinations entered, teacher qualifications (allowing for non-qualified and non-graduate teachers), and meeting of fire regulations. (They can be struck off the register if they do not comply.) Registration is provisional until accommodation and premises are inspected.[14] There is also a complaints procedure set up, heard by the Independent Schools Tribunal.

---

[14] Under the Inspection of Premises, Children and Records (Independent Schools) Regulations 1991.

Realistically, however, there would be greater demands for accountability, as these educational settings will be in receipt of public funds. There is a precedent I wish to use here. Independent schools receiving funds from the Assisted Places Scheme only have to go through the normal registration process, and furnish audited accounts.[15] Could not a similar process be used for the new educational settings? It could of course be argued that the Assisted Places schools receive *most* of their funds from the market, and hence have accountability ensured in this way. Perhaps this principle could be extended to those educational settings which are to receive funds from LIFE accounts? If the majority of their funds is received from private sources, then all they need to do is to register as an Independent School to be able to receive LIFE funds. However, if they receive the majority of their funds from public sources, then they would need to register and, as well, undergo a rigorous inspection, similar to that endured by state schools. This need not mean an inspection by the state agency, Ofsted.[16] There is an inspection service within the private sector – the Independent Schools Joint Council (ISJC) Accreditation Service – which, under the recent Deregulation Act, finds itself able to inspect private schools; this body may well be able to compete with the state agency, providing 'responsible self-regulation' (Hearnden, 1995). Clearly, any inspection would take into account the specialised nature of the setting being inspected. If at any time a setting moved from having the majority of its funds private to the majority public, or vice versa, then the inspection requirement would be adjusted accordingly.

There is also another very important precedent which can be used to ensure liberation of the supply-side of these new settings, regarding qualified teachers. City Technology Colleges (CTCs), set up by the government to provide beacons of technological excellence primarily in the inner cities, with capital costs partly financed by industry, are known as 'independent state schools'. Although they receive *all* their current spending from government, they are treated as genuine independent schools when it comes to their teaching

---

[15] Education (Assisted Places) Regulations 1989.

[16] Office of Standards in Education, which replaced Her Majesty's Inspectorate (HMI).

staff. The headteacher and governors are allowed to employ anyone they deem suitable for teaching, as are independent schools, whether or not he or she has a teaching qualification, and whether or not they are graduates. This principle would be extended to the new educational settings in receipt of LIFE funds. The important qualification for any teaching job would be the desire to teach, and appropriate knowledge and skills gained from any source, not the level of paper qualifications offered.

Opting Out of Centralised Control

It might be thought that these new educational institutions or settings would need to follow relevant parts of the National Curriculum, national testing, and be included in the compulsory league tables. This would be disastrous, and indeed, for moves towards markets, all of these centralising measures need to be undermined, for all schools. As it happens, to permit opting out of the National Curriculum would not require any new legislation. Hidden away in the 1988 Education Reform Act are the little-noticed Sections 16 and 17. Section 16 permits schools to apply to the Secretary of State to opt out of the National Curriculum, in part or in whole. Section 17 allows the Secretary of State to authorise *any* departure from the National Curriculum, by regulation. So we could envisage something like a *'standard track'* to opting out of the National Curriculum, using Section 16, with a *'fast-track'* using Section 17.

For the standard track route, the existing legislation itself is all that is required – no new regulations or orders are needed. For Section 16 presents, *as it stands*, a clear, unambiguous loophole in the application of the National Curriculum. The clause reads that, for the purpose of 'development work' or 'experiments', schools are permitted to apply to the Secretary of State for Education to opt out of the curriculum, and these are sufficiently broad terms to cover a variety of eventualities. Almost *any* change to a school's curriculum can be described as 'development work', as was acknowledged by the Government in the Act's passage through Parliament. So no new legislation is required and schools could, right now, start to use this process to opt out. What would aid the process, however, would be for the Government to publicise the existence of Section 16, and for schools to be reassured that applications will be sympathetically handled. Upon opting out of the National Curriculum, a proportion of the budget of the Schools Curriculum and Assessment Authority (SCAA) – the curriculum quango – could be allocated to the school, for purposes of curriculum development and assessment.

Under the 'fast-track' route, the Secretary of State for Education would, by regulation, create a category of schools named the 'Innovative Curriculum' (IC) schools. This category describes schools which are either (a) over-subscribed, or (b) have sufficient demand to fill all their pupil places at age 14. By specifying such schools under regulation, the Secretary of State can then use Section 17 of the 1988 Education Reform Act to allow for the National Curriculum not to apply to IC schools for ages 14 and above. Schools fulfilling either of the specified requirements would then be invited – there would be no compulsion – to apply for IC status. On application by the governing body of the school, a simple checking procedure quickly evaluates the school's records, and, if its claim is confirmed, opting out is permitted without fuss. As with Section 16 opt-outs, a proportion of the budget of SCAA would be given to the school.

The advantages that these proposals would bring to schools are clear: schools which were popular, or had visionary leaders or innovative staff, would be released from the burden of following a centrally prescribed curriculum, and from the associated and cumbersome administrative tasks which accompany it; those schools would also receive additional funds devolved from central government. Meanwhile, those schools which were not in the position to demonstrate their popularity, or who did not wish to be innovative around their curriculum, could still follow the National Curriculum. So, again, we see the establishment of voluntary mechanisms to allow schools to move away from centralising state control, while those that do not wish to can remain within the current arrangements. Of course, new educational settings in receipt of LIFE funds could follow the National Curriculum if they wished – as, indeed, some independent schools are doing. However, there would be no compulsion for them to do so.

Allowing opting out of the league tables and national testing would require new legislation (although since opting out of the National Curriculum is allowed, there is an obvious logic to permitting this to happen, as the National Curriculum is the syllabus of national testing, and the league tables will increasingly depend upon these examination results).

Do Markets in Education Need Centralised Curriculum Control?

There are some who will be surprised that these moves should be advocated in this paper. Both critics and supporters have tried to rationalise the incongruity of the government's centralising measures in the context of the market. Chitty was one of the first to argue that informed parental choice requires a national curriculum:

> 'the [National] Curriculum does, after all, act as justification for a massive programme of national testing at 7, 11, 14 and 16 which will, in turn, provide evidence to parents for the desirability or otherwise of individual schools' (Chitty, 1989, p.218).

Markets can only work effectively, he argues, if there is 'maximum consumer information'.

This objection is not quite right, however. It applies one model of economic theory – the neo-classical theory of perfect competition. In a perfectly competitive market it is true that perfect knowledge would be needed. But perfectly competitive markets do not exist in the real world, they are (to the neo-classical economists) simply a useful model on which to make predictions. The model implicit throughout this paper has been Hayek's 'Austrian' model, where there is uncertainty about consumer tastes and preferences, and where the market acts as a discovery mechanism. No perfect information is required here. But even if we would wish to adopt the neo-classical model, we could see how, in reality, national testing could not possibly provide the information required. For it is not possible to have totally reliable and valid tests, nor is it possible to analyse these results in a way that truly reflects the 'value-added' by the school. Moreover, not many would want to argue that such tests genuinely reflect all that is educationally valuable in schools. So what we are left with is that the information from national testing is, at best, very imperfect, and, at worst, positively misleading (because of unreliability, invalidity, and no accurate means of presenting value-added).

106

Given these imperfections, it appears that for the imperfect market of educational provision, the consumers need information, but that, as in any other market, this information can be acquired through various 'imperfect' mechanisms. National testing derived from a national curriculum could be one of these, but because of its expense and inconvenience is unlikely to be rated highly compared with other measures. These could include considerations of a school's informal reputation, observations of pupils in the school and in the neighbourhood, subjective evaluations about appearance of school, discipline reputation, and so on. It may be that consumer organisations would decide that examination results are of importance, and they might publish statistical *sample* surveys of schools, even sample standardised tests. But to suppose that, just because there is a market, this requires standardised *national* testing, is a serious misunderstanding of the nature of the market.

The absurdity of this position can be clearly realised, indeed, if instead of education we consider other markets. Is Chitty (1989) suggesting, for example, that when we buy clothes, or food, or other consumer goods, we are being deprived because we cannot consult national government league tables? Presumably not. We rely on many different ways of buying goods, including reputation, advertising and independent consumer reports; but no-one expects the sorts of detailed information that the Government is trying to impose upon schools now. The argument from Chapter 5 has suggested that there are no important differences between education and other goods in this crucial respect at least.

To put it in a slightly more concrete form, consider a school which is not doing at all well at present, like Moston Park in Manchester where 51 per cent of young people leave with *no examination passes at all*. The league tables have one, temporary, use – they do enable many of us to see that such schools exist, and that there are such dire problems with state schooling (although a research project could, of course, also have discovered this). But for bringing improvements to the failing school, observe how they push it in a direction which may not be desirable. To improve its position, Moston Park would have to concentrate its resources on making sure that more children gained some grades in GCSEs – History, Geography, Science, and so on. However, perhaps a better target for the school would be to expend its energies on developing employable young people, whether or not they have GCSEs, which many employers do not necessarily seek if youngsters have other qualities. Or perhaps on developing self-employment skills, so that the young people do not have to be dependent on an unfriendly job market. Or perhaps developing functional literacy and numeracy should be the most important goal.

The key point is that, from a distance, we really do not know what Moston Park should be doing, but that there are people there who will have a clearer notion, and can experiment and innovate if they are free to do so, and have the appropriate incentives. Of course, it could be argued that this leaves failing schools not to expect much from young people, to acquiesce in their decline. This is a risk, but in a world of trade-offs, it is a lesser risk than bringing in measures and standards which may be singularly inappropriate. Moreover, the importance of the earlier demand-side reforms must not be ignored in bringing about the sort of accountability that national testing and league tables are supposed to bring. If the school is providing something totally inappropriate, its 14-year-olds will leave *en masse* – and will not need a Secretary of State for Education to have to intervene in order to close it. A position at the bottom of the league table is not required to reinforce *that* sort of accountability.

However, in some circles there is great attachment to national league tables. Perhaps schools which opt out of them could be encouraged (but not compelled) to develop alternative 'accountability' measures which might go some way to satisfy those who like to see performance more objectively measured. One possible method which, in any case, there would be market incentives to develop, would be a measure of how many young people left school and within a defined period were gainfully employed, self-employed, or in further or higher education. It should not be too difficult to calculate such measures to a fair degree of approximation, and these could be a valuable marketing tool for schools. '82 per cent of our school graduates find work within six months' would be a proud advertisement for any Moston Park, and surely more appropriate than 'x per cent of our graduates obtain five or more GCSEs'.

Moreover, particularly innovative schools might include a money-back guarantee to individuals who failed to find employment or further education. To these ends such schools would be aware of the value of employing 'work liaison officers', who actively sought to build up links with employers, to help find employment for their students. In this way, the gulf between employers and schools could be further broken down.

Waiving Other Rules

The final aspect of the supply-side reforms would be to waive two sets of rules which currently impose constraints on moves towards an educational market. The rules which forbid schools to borrow on their assets need to be scrapped to allow increased private finance to be brought into primary and secondary education.[17] There are already exciting examples of what is possible within the current régime. One school (Sawtry Community College, Huntingdon), for example, is leasing surplus school accommodation for a crèche. A private company pays the school rent, and runs the crèche, which is then open for use by teachers, parents and the wider community. Another school (Garibaldi School, Mansfield) turned under-utilised library space into a commercial conference centre, rented out to the private sector at weekends, and a national network of translators uses office space in a newly-built language centre. These types of initiatives should be encouraged; allowing schools to borrow on their assets would permit even more exciting developments to take off.

The second set of rules would be those which discourage new state schools from being opened if there are 'surplus places' in the system. At present, this particularly affects educational entrepreneurs who wish to open new schools under the 1993 Education Act (which allows private schools to opt in to GM status, and new schools to receive 85 per cent of their capital costs if they do so). The rules do allow for new schools if they can demonstrate that they fill some niche which is not being met – for example, if they are religious schools in an area without such schools. But markets need

---

[17] There may be legislation forthcoming to waive these rules for grant-maintained schools; this should be amended to include all schools.

entrepreneurs to be able to open new supply whenever *they* think there is potential demand, irrespective of the penchants of local or national bureaucrats. It would be desirable if this rule could be relaxed for all schools. It is imperative that it is not a factor in the registration of new educational settings seeking to capture demand brought about by the LIFE reform.

Towards Privatisation, Towards Liberation

Markets get a bad press in educational circles. The main purpose of this paper has been to show that this is undeserved, and to shift the terms of the educational policy debate. The debate tends to become entangled in the parochialism of government policy; it avoids confronting the larger issue of whether governments should be involved in education in the first place, and if so, to what extent that involvement is morally justifiable. This is the crucial question of education policy for the new millennium. It is the crucial question for those concerned for children stuck in state schools which are failing them in every sense of the term. But it also is the crucial question for all those who want to see the development of a society where learning is a pleasure for all. Through markets, life-long learning will be taken on eagerly by those who have not had the joy of learning stamped out of them by the clumsily inflexible circumstances of their compulsory schooling. The debate about markets is fundamentally a debate about the desirable extent of government intervention in education. This debate should not become so caught up in exposing any disadvantages of the so-called market – the still heavily interventionist state system – that it remains blinded to the potential of the market solution to educational problems.

With a lowered school-leaving age and funds in a LIFE account, young people could at last begin to express their genuine educational needs and requirements; with private funds invested, enterprise and initiative creatively harnessed, a diversity of schools and other educational opportunities could emerge to serve this demand. But the proposals do not force change if change is not desired. They are not imposing 'the dogma of the market' on anyone, only allowing the market to cultivate an environment in which educational needs can be discovered and development nurtured. Most importantly, the proposals do not take us towards something to be feared.

Markets in education are justified in terms of equity and democracy. For too long government intervention has deadened and subdued the enterprise of education. Moving towards markets will enliven and liberate the educational endeavour.

References/Bibliography

Anderson, Terry L., and Donald R. Leal (1991): *Free Market Environmentalism*, Boulder, Colorado: Westview Press.

Apps, Jerold W. (1988): *Higher Education in a Learning Society*, San Francisco, CA: Jossey-Bass Publishers.

Ball, Christopher (1993): Towards a Learning Society: Making Sense of the Reform and Restructuring of Education and Training in the UK (Work-in-progress), London: Royal Society of Arts.

Ball, Stephen J. (1990a): *Markets, Morality and Equality in Education*, Hillcole Group Paper 5, London: The Tufnell Press.

Ball, Stephen J. (1990b): 'Education, Inequality and School Reform: Values in Crisis', Inaugural Lecture, Centre for Educational Studies, King's College London, University of London, 15 October.

Ball, Stephen J. (1990c): *Politics and Policy Making In Education*, London: Routledge.

Barber, Michael (1994): 'Power and Control in Education 1944-2004', *British Journal of Educational Studies*, Vol.42, No.4, pp.348-62.

Barnett, Ronald (1992): 'The Learning Society?', *Reflections on Higher Education*, Vol.4, pp.70-75.

Barr, Nicholas ([1987], 1993): *The Economics of the Welfare State*, London: Weidenfeld and Nicolson.

Barrow, Robin (1987): 'Skill Talk', *Journal of Philosophy of Education*, Vol.21(2), pp.187-96.

Barrow, Robin (1990): *Understanding Skills*, London, Ontario: The Althouse Press.

Bash, Leslie, and David Coulby (1989): *The Education Reform Act: Competition and Control*, London: Cassell Education.

Bate, Roger, and Julian Morris (1994): *Global Warming: Apocalypse or Hot Air?*, IEA Studies on the Environment No.1, London: Institute of Economic Affairs Environment Unit.

Bierhoff, Helva, and S.J. Prais (1995): *Schooling as Preparation for life and work in Switzerland and Britain*, Discussion Paper No.75, London: National Institute of Economic and Social Research.

Brown, F. (1995): 'Privatization of Public Education: Theories and Concepts', in *Education and Urban Society*, Vol.27(2): Richard C. Hunter and Frank Brown (eds.), *Privatization in Public Education*, Special Edition, February.

Cato, Vivienne, and Chris Whetton (1991): *An Enquiry into Local Education Authority Evidence on Standards of Reading of Seven Year Old Children*, London: Department of Education and Science.

Central Statistical Office (1995): *Social Trends: 1995 Edition*, London: HMSO.

Chitty, Clyde (1989): *Towards a New Education System: The Victory of the New Right?*, Lewes: Falmer Press.

Chubb, John E., and Terry M. Moe (1990): *Politics, Markets and America's Schools*, Washington DC: The Brookings Institution.

Chubb, John E., and Terry M. Moe (1992): *A Lesson in School Reform from Great Britain*, Washington DC: The Brookings Institution.

Coleman, J.S., *et al.* (1966): *Equality of Educational Opportunity*, Washington, DC: US Government.

Commission on Social Justice (1994): *Social Justice: Strategies for National Renewal*, London: Institute for Public Policy Research.

Cowen, Tyler (1992): 'Public Goods and Externalities: Old and New Perspectives', in Tyler Cowen (ed.), *Public Goods & Market Failures: A Critical Examination*, New Brunswick: Transaction Publishers.

Davis, Evan (1993): *Schools and the State*, London: Social Market Foundation.

De Jasay, Anthony (1990): *Market Socialism: A Scrutiny – 'This Square Circle'*, Occasional Paper No.84, London: Institute of Economic Affairs.

Department for Education and Employment (1995): *Lifetime Learning: a Consultation Document*, London: HMSO.

Dore, Ronald (1976): *The Diploma Disease*, London: George Allen and Unwin.

Drucker, Peter (1993): *Post-capitalist Society*, Oxford: Butterworth-Heinemann.

Dworkin, Ronald (1981a): 'What is Equality? Part 1: Equality of Welfare', *Philosophy & Public Affairs*, Vol.10, pp.185-246.

Dworkin, Ronald (1981b): 'What is Equality? Part 2: Equality of Resources', *Philosophy & Public Affairs*, Vol.10, pp.283-345.

Dworkin, Ronald (1983): 'Comment on Narveson: In Defense of Equality', *Social Philosophy and Policy*, Vol.1, pp.24-40.

Dworkin, Ronald (1985): 'Why Liberals Should Care About Equality', in Ronald Dworkin, *A Matter of Principle*, Cambridge, Mass.: Harvard University Press.

Dworkin, Ronald (1987): 'What is Equality? Part 3: The Place of Liberty', *Iowa Law Review*, Vol.73, pp.1-27.

Dworkin, Ronald (1988): 'What Is Equality? Part 4: Political Equality', *University of San Francisco Law Review*, Vol.22, pp.1-30.

Flew, Antony (1976): *Sociology, Equality and Education: Philosophical Essays in Defence of a Variety of Differences*, London: Macmillan.

Flew, Antony (1981): *The Politics of Procrustes: Contradictions of Enforced Equality*, London: Temple Smith.

Flew, Antony (1995): *All the Right Places*, London: Adam Smith Institute.

Fogelman, Ken (ed.) (1991): *Citizenship in Schools*, London: David Fulton.

Frankfurt, Harry G. (1988): *The Importance of What We Care About: Philosophical Essays*, Cambridge: Cambridge University Press.

Friedman, Milton, and Rose Friedman (1980): *Free to Choose*, New York: Harcourt, Brace, Jovanovich.

Gardner, Philip (1984): *The Lost Elementary Schools of Victorian England: The People's Education*, London: Croom Helm.

Garforth, F.W. (1980): *Educative Democracy: John Stuart Mill on Education in Society*, Oxford: Oxford University Press.

Gatto, John Taylor (1990): *Dumbing us Down: the Hidden Curriculum of Compulsory Schooling*, Philadelphia: New Society.

Goodin, R.E., and Julian Le Grand (1987): *Not Only the Poor: The Middle Classes and the Welfare State*, London: Allen and Unwin.

Grace, Gerald (1989): 'Education: Commodity or Public Good?', *British Journal of Educational Studies*, Vol.37, pp.207-11.

Gray, John (1992): *The Moral Foundations of Market Institutions*, Choice in Welfare No.10, London: Institute of Economic Affairs Health and Welfare Unit.

Green, Andy (1990): *Education and State Formation*, Basingstoke and London: Macmillan.

Green, Andy (1991): 'The Structure of the System: Proposals for Change', in Clyde Chitty (ed.), *Changing the Future: Redprint for Education*, The Hillcole Group, London: The Tufnell Press.

Griffiths, Morwenna (1987): 'The Teaching of Skills and the Skills of Teaching', *Journal of Philosophy of Education*, Vol.21(2), pp.203-14.

Halil, Tony, and David J. Whitehead (1990): 'Economic Literacy in the UK and the USA: An Empirical Analysis', *Economics*, Vol.26, No.1, pp.33-38.

Hargreaves, David (1994): *The Mosaic of Learning*, London: Demos.

Hayek, F.A. (1960): *The Constitution of Liberty*, London: Routledge & Kegan Paul.

Hayek, F.A. (1978): *New Studies in Philosophy, Politics, Economics and the History of Ideas*, London: Routledge & Kegan Paul.

Hayek, F.A. (1982): *Law, Legislation and Liberty* (3 vols.), collected edition, London: Routledge & Kegan Paul.

Hearnden, Arthur (1995): 'Independence and Deregulation', *ISJC Bulletin*, No.23, p.1.

High, Jack, and Jerome Ellig (1992): 'The Private Supply of Education: Some Historical Evidence', in Tyler Cowen (ed.), *Public Goods & Market Failures: A Critical Examination*, New Brunswick: Transaction Publishers.

Hirschman, A.O. (1970): *Exit, Voice and Loyalty: Responses to Decline in Firms, Organisations and States*, Cambridge, Mass.: Harvard University Press.

Husén, Torsten (1974): *The Learning Society*, London: Methuen.

Husén, Torsten (1986): *The Learning Society Revisited*, Oxford: Pergamon Press.

Hutchins, Robert (1968): *The Learning Society*, New York: New York American Library.

Industry in Education (1996): *Towards employability: Addressing the gap between young people's qualities and employers' recruitment needs*, London: Industry in Education.

Jencks, C., *et al.* (1971): *Inequality*, London: Allen Lane.

Johnson, Richard (1979): '"Really Useful Knowledge": Radical Education and Working Class Culture, 1790-1848', in John Clarke, Chas. Critcher and Richard Johnson (eds.), *Working Class Culture: Studies in History and Theory*, London: Hutchinson.

Jonathan, Ruth (1989): 'Choice and Control in Education: Parental Rights, Individual Liberties and Social Justice', *British Journal of Educational Studies*, Vol.37, pp.321-38.

Jonathan, Ruth (1990): 'State Education Service or Prisoner's Dilemma: The "Hidden Hand" as Source of Education Policy', *British Journal of Educational Studies*, Vol.38, pp.116-32.

Kiesling, Herbert J. (1983): 'Nineteenth-Century Education According to West: A Comment', *Economic History Review*, Vol.36, pp.416-25.

Kiesling, Herbert J. (1990): 'Pedagogical Uses of the Public Goods Concept in Economics', *Journal of Economic Education*, Vol.21, pp.137-47.

Le Grand, Julian, and Ray Robinson (eds.) (1984): *Privatisation and the Welfare State*, London: George Allen and Unwin.

Le Grand, Julian (1982): 'The Distribution of Public Expenditure on Education', *Economica*, Vol.49, pp.63-68.

Le Grand, Julian (1991): *Equity and Choice: An Essay in Economics and Applied Philosophy*, London: HarperCollins.

Levitas, Ruth (1986): 'Competition and Compliance: The Utopias of the New Right', in Ruth Levitas (ed.), *The Ideology of the New Right*, Cambridge: Polity Press.

Lott, John R. (1987a): 'Why is Education Publicly Provided? A Critical Survey', *Cato Journal*, Vol.7, pp.475-501.

Lott, John R. (1987b): 'Juvenile Delinquency and Education: A Comparison of Public and Private Provision', *International Review of Law and Economics*, Vol.7, pp.163-75.

Marks, John, and Maciej Pomian-Srzednicki (1985): *Standards in English Schools: Second Report*, London: National Council for Educational Standards.

Marks, John, Caroline Cox, and Maciej Pomian-Srzednicki (1986): *Examination Performance of Secondary Schools in the Inner London Education Authority*, London: National Council for Educational Standards.

Miliband, David (1991): *Markets, Politics and Education: Beyond the Education Reform Act*, London: Institute for Public Policy Research.

Mill, John Stuart ([1859], 1972): *On Liberty*, London: J.M. Dent.

Mill, John Stuart ([1861], 1972): *Utilitarianism, On Liberty and Considerations on Representative Government*, London: J.M. Dent.

Morris, Julian (1995): *The Political Economy of Land Degradation*, IEA Studies on the Environment No.5, London: Institute of Economic Affairs Environment Unit.

Mortimore, Peter (1995): *Effective Schools: Current Impact and Future Potential*, London: Institute of Education.

Mulligan, Jim (1994): *No Limit: A Blueprint for Involving Volunteers in Schools*, London: Community Service Volunteers.

Murray, Charles (1994): *In Pursuit: Of Happiness and Good Government*, San Francisco, CA: Institute for Contemporary Studies.

National Commission on Education (1993): *Learning to Succeed: A Radical Look at Education Today and a Strategy for the Future*, London: NCE.

National Commission on Education (1994): *Learning to Succeed: The Way Ahead*, London: NCE.

Narveson, Jan (1983): 'On Dworkinian Equality', *Social Philosophy and Policy*, Vol.1, pp.1-23.

Oakeshott, Michael (1962): *Rationalism in Politics and Other Essays*, London: Methuen.

Ofsted (1995): *Annual Report of Her Majesty's Chief Inspector of Schools: Part 1. Standards and Quality in Education 1993/94*, London: HMSO.

O'Hear, Philip, and John White (1991): *A National Curriculum for All: Laying the Foundations for Success*, London: Institute for Public Policy Research.

Osterfield, David (1992): *Prosperity versus Planning: How Government Stifles Economic Growth*, New York: Oxford University Press.

Peacock, Alan T., and Jack Wiseman (1964): *Education for Democrats*, Hobart Paper No.25, London: Institute of Economic Affairs.

Polanyi, Michael (1958): *Personal Knowledge*, London: Routledge & Kegan Paul.

Pring, Richard (1994): 'Liberal and Vocational Education: A Conflict of Value', in John Haldane (ed.), *Education, Values and the State*, St. Andrews: Centre for Philosophy and Public Affairs.

Ranson, Stewart (1990): 'From 1944 to 1988: Education, Citizenship and Democracy', in M. Flude and M. Hammer (eds.), *The Education Reform Act 1988: Its Origins and Implications*, Lewes: The Falmer Press.

Ranson, Stewart (1992): 'Towards the Learning Society', *Educational Management and Administration*, Vol.20(2), April, pp.68-79.

Ranson, Stewart (1993): 'Markets or Democracy for Education', *British Journal of Educational Studies*, Vol.41, pp.333-52.

Ranson, Stewart (1994): *Towards the Learning Society*, London: Cassell.

Rawls, John (1972): *A Theory of Justice*, Oxford: Clarendon Press.

Raz, Joseph (1986): *The Morality of Freedom*, Oxford: Clarendon Press.

Reid, T. Wemyss ([1888], 1970): *Life of the Rt. Hon. W.E. Forster*, New York: Augustus M. Kelley.

Reynolds, D. (1982): 'The Search for Effective Schools', *School Organisation*, Vol.2(3), pp.215-37.

Richman, Sheldon (1994): *Separating School and State*, Fairfax, VA: The Future of Freedom Foundation.

Rutter, Michael, Barbara Maughan, Peter Mortimore, Janet Ouston (1979): *Fifteen Thousand Hours*, London: Open Books.

Rutter, Michael, and David J. Smith (1995): *Psychosocial Disorders in Young People: Time Trends and their Causes*, Chichester: John Wiley.

Seldon, Arthur (1986): *The Riddle of the Voucher*, Hobart Paperback No.21, London: Institute of Economic Affairs.

Seldon, Arthur (1990): *Capitalism*, Oxford: Basil Blackwell.

Smith, David J., and Sally Tomlinson (1989): *The School Effect: A Study of Multi-Racial Comprehensives*, London: Policy Studies Institute.

Smith, Richard (1987): 'Skills: the Middle Way', *Journal of Philosophy of Education*, Vol.21(2), pp.197-202.

Sowell, Thomas (1980): *Knowledge and Decisions*, New York: Basic Books.

Stephens, W.B. (1987): *Education, Literacy and Society 1830-70: the Geography of Diversity in Provincial England*, Manchester: Manchester University Press.

Thatcher, Margaret (1993): *The Downing Street Years*, London: HarperCollins.

Tooley, James (1994): 'In Defence of Markets in Education', in David Bridges and Terry McLaughlin (eds.), *Education and the Market Place*, London: Falmer.

Tooley, James (1995a): *Disestablishing the School*, Aldershot: Avebury.

Tooley, James (1995b): 'Markets or Democracy for Education? A Reply to Stewart Ranson', *British Journal of Educational Studies*, Vol.43, No.1, pp.21-34.

Tooley, James (1995c): Review of Walford, Geoffrey (1994), in *Cambridge Journal of Education*, Vol.25, No.3, pp.384-86.

Tooley, James (1996): 'Cooperation without Deliberation: the Market Solution', in Keith Watson (ed.), *Educational Dilemmas*, London: Cassell.

University of North London, Truancy Unit (1994): *Truancy in English Secondary Schools*, A Report prepared for the DFE by the Truancy Research Project, London: HMSO.

Walford, Geoffrey (1994): *Choice and Equity in Education*, London: Cassell.

Watts, A.G., and P. Moran (eds.) (1984): *Education for Enterprise*, London: Open University Press.

West, E.G. (1970): 'Resource Allocation and Growth in Early Nineteenth Century British Education', *Economic History Review*, Vol.XXIII, pp.68-95.

West, E.G. (1975): *Nonpublic School Aid*, Lexington, MA: D.C. Heath.

West, E.G. (1983): 'Nineteenth-Century Educational History: The Kiesling Critique', *Economic History Review*, Vol.36, pp.426-34.

West, E.G. (1986): 'An Economic Rationale for Public Schools: The Search Continues', *Teachers College Record*, Vol.88, pp.152-62.

West, E.G. ([1965], 1994a): *Education and the State* (3rd edition), Indianapolis: Liberty Fund (1st and 2nd editions, IEA, London).

West, E.G. (1994b): 'Education Without the State', *Economic Affairs*, Vol.14, No.5, pp.12-15.

White, John (1990): *Education and the Good Life*, London: Kogan Page.

White, John (1994): 'Education and the Limits of the Market', in David Bridges and Terry McLaughlin (eds.), *Education and the Market Place*, London: Falmer.

White, John (1995): 'The Dishwasher's Child: Education and the End of Egalitarianism', *Journal of Philosophy of Education*, Vol.28, No.2, pp.173-81.